Psalms

JEROME F. D. CREACH

WESTMINSTER
JOHN KNOX PRESS
LOUISVILLE · KENTUCKY

Scripture quotations, unless otherwise noted, are from the New Revised Standard Version of the Bible, copyright © 1989 by the Division of Christian Education of the National Council of the Churches of Christ in the U.S.A., and are used by permission.

The photographs on pages 1, 18, 26, 27, 31, 36, 42, 50, 65, 70, 74, 77, 83, 86, and 93 are © 1998 PhotoDisc, Inc. All rights reserved. Used by permission.

The photographs on pages 60 and 62 are used by permission of The Fellowship for Readers of the Urantia Book.

The illustration on page 39, *The Return of the Prodigal Son,* by Rembrandt Harmensz van Rijn, is reproduced by permission of the Fine Arts Museums of San Francisco, the Achenbach Foundation for Graphic Arts, Bruno and Sadie Adriani Collection, 1963.30.183.

Book design by Drew Stevens
Cover design by Pam Poll
Cover illustration Robert Stratton

First edition
Published by Westminster John Knox Press
Louisville, Kentucky

This book is printed on acid-free paper that meets the American National Standards Institute Z39.48 standard. ∞

PRINTED IN THE UNITED STATES OF AMERICA

10 11 12 — 10 9 8 7

Library of Congress Cataloging-in-Publication Data

A catalog record for this book is available from the Library of Congress.

ISBN-13: 978-0-664-22600-8
ISBN-10: 0-664-22600-0

Psalms

INTERPRETATION
BIBLE STUDIES

Contents

Series Introduction

The Bible long has been revered for its witness to God's presence and re-deeming activity in the world; its message of creation and judgment, love and forgiveness, grace and hope; its memorable characters and stories; its challenges to human life; and its power to shape faith. For generations people have found in the Bible inspiration and instruction, and, for nearly as long, commentators and scholars have assisted students of the Bible. This series, Interpretation Bible Studies (IBS), continues that great heritage of scholarship with a fresh approach to biblical study.

Designed for ease and flexibility of use for either personal or group study, IBS helps readers not only to learn about the history and theology of the Bible, understand the sometimes difficult language of biblical passages, and marvel at the biblical accounts of God's activity in human life, but also to accept the challenge of the Bible's call to discipleship. IBS offers sound guidance for deepening one's knowledge of the Bible and for faithful Christian living in today's world.

IBS was developed out of three primary convictions. First, the Bible is the church's scripture and stands in a unique place of authority in Christian understanding. Second, good scholarship helps readers understand the truths of the Bible and sharpens their perception of God speaking through the Bible. Third, deep knowledge of the Bible bears fruit in one's ethical and spiritual life.

Each IBS volume has ten brief units of key passages from a book of the Bible. By moving through these units, readers capture the sweep of the whole biblical book. Each unit includes study helps, such as maps, photos, definitions of key terms, questions for reflection, and suggestions for resources for further study. In the back of each volume is a Leader's Guide that offers helpful suggestions on how to use IBS.

The Interpretation Bible Studies series grows out of the well-known Interpretation commentaries (John Knox Press), a series that helps preachers and teachers in their preparation. Although each IBS volume bears a deep kinship to its companion Interpretation commentary, IBS can stand alone. The reader need not be familiar with the Interpretation commentary to benefit from IBS. However, those who want to discover even more about the Bible will benefit by consulting Interpretation commentaries too.

Through the kind of encounter with the Bible encouraged by the Interpretation Bible Studies, the church will continue to discover God speaking afresh in the scriptures.

Introduction to Psalms

The following studies of the book of Psalms serve as a companion to James L. Mays, *Psalms,* Interpretation: A Bible Commentary for Teaching and Preaching (Louisville, Ky.: John Knox Press, 1994). When ideas, words, or phrases are borrowed directly from Mays, a parenthetical page reference is given. Look to that commentary for additional discussion of the issues and for treatment of psalms not covered here. The most important references in these studies, however, are to the Bible itself. Therefore, keep an open Bible nearby. May the following comments open windows of understanding in study of the book of Psalms, and simultaneously provide a sense of awe at one of the great treasures of scripture.

A lyre

The Title of the Book

There are two well-known titles for the book of Psalms. The English title, "Psalms," comes from a Greek word that refers to songs accompanied by stringed instruments. A similar word, "Psalter," derives from another Greek term that denotes the stringed instrument itself, probably the lyre (see 1 Sam. 16:14–23), and provides another popular name for the book. These two titles indicate that most psalms were written for corporate worship. Appropriately then, the

1

church throughout its history has used psalms as lyrics for hymns as well as liturgy for recitation.

The Psalter contains a variety of types of psalms that can be used in many occasions in the life of the church. However, the book actually is dominated by prayers that complain to God about a specific dire situation of an individual or group. This seems puzzling because a third popular title for the Psalms is the Hebrew word, *Tehillim*, which means "praises." Apparently all the Psalms, even those filled with raw anger and discontent, were understood as instruments of praise. This view of the Psalter is not a naive avoidance of the book's sharper edges; rather, the Hebrew title grows out of a recognition that every address to God is founded in faith and trust in God.

> "The wide range of expression in the Psalter—the anger and pain of lament, the anguished self-probing of confession, the grateful fervor of thanksgiving, the ecstatic joy of praise—allows us to bring our whole lives before God." —Kathleen Norris, *The Psalms*, viii.

Nature of Prayer in the Psalms

In addition to providing a vocabulary for liturgical prayers (i.e., calls to worship, prayers of confessions, responsive readings, etc.), the Psalms have been used for ages as model prayers for Christians. The Psalter itself encourages the use of the poems this way, as shown in unit 1, "The Anatomy of a Psalm." However, in order to make the prayers of the Psalter truly *our* prayers, two important characteristics of the Psalms should be kept in mind: first, the psalms were not prayed privately or in isolation. When an individual speaks in a psalm, he or she prays from within a congregation, or on behalf of a group. Christian prayer that imitates that of the psalmists "binds the saints across the ages and frees them from isolation and arbitrary autonomy in prayer" (Mays, 2). Praying with the Psalms as models can aid in that endeavor.

> "When one sits alone with a Psalm, one is sitting with and for the countless others who are praying them now, who have prayed them for thousands of years." —Kathleen Norris, *The Psalms*, x.

Second, many of the Psalms speak from the depths of great suffering, oppression, and persecution. Most North American Christians may be ill suited to pray such prayers, given the religious and political freedom and prosperity of their part of the world. It is appropriate, however, to pray these prayers *on behalf of*

2

others. Such praying can bind the spirits of the more privileged with those of the poor or oppressed of the world, be they Christians in China, the poor of Latin America, or Holocaust victims. This perspective in prayer avoids cheapening and reducing the passion of psalmic lament and complaint, and by learning to pray on behalf of others, one enters a fruitful tradition of prayer that is too often lost on the imperious individualism of Western Christianity.

Structure of the Book of Psalms

The book of Psalms consists of 150 individual poems. Many of these, particularly in the first half of the book, are organized in collections that bear in their titles the name of figures associated with the worship of ancient Israel (David, Korah, Asaph). The Psalter,

> **Who are these guys?**
>
> *Korah*—The leader of a Levite clan (Ex. 6:21) of Temple gatekeepers (1 Chron. 9:19) and singers (2 Chron. 20:19).
>
> *Asaph*—A music leader appointed by David (1 Chron. 6:39) and a member of a Levite clan responsible for the bread of the Presence offered to God in the Temple (1 Chron. 9:32).

then, is a kind of "collection of collections," along with the addition of some untitled works that apparently existed independent of an individual collection until they became part of the present Psalter.

Psalms 41; 72; 89; and 106 end with similar doxological formulas including the word "amen." These lines help divide the Psalter into five sections or "books" (Psalms 1–41; 42–72; 73–89; 90–106; 107–150) with Psalm 150 serving as a final doxology for the whole collection. The fivefold division undoubtedly is meant to reflect an imitation of the Torah (Genesis–Deuteronomy).

Psalms 1 and 2 together serve as an introduction and offer guidance on how the whole Psalter should be read. A common vocabulary unites these two psalms. One of the most obvious unifying features is the expression, "Happy is . . ." (Pss. 1:1; 2:12). In both psalms this line describes the righteous person. The psalms that follow, then, offer an extended portrait of the righteous, and invite all to live in ways that will characterize them as "happy."

The Theology of the Psalms

The diversity of the psalms makes it impossible to sketch a systematic theology of the Psalter. There are some recurring themes, however, that are at the heart of the faith presented in the psalms. At the center of its beliefs about God is the Psalter's claim that "the LORD reigns" (Mays, 30–31), and "King" is the most prominent metaphor for God in the Psalms. All other roles of God (warrior, judge, savior, shepherd, refuge, creator) are to be understood as a part of God's role as king.

> "The psalms are the poetry of the reign of the LORD." —James L. Mays, *Psalms*, Interpretation, 30.

According to the Psalms, the Lord reigns from a chosen "capital," Mount Zion (Ps. 46:4–7; 48:1–3; 76:1–3; 122:3–5). From that locale, the divine King issues decrees, commands, and statutes called *torah* (see Isa. 2:3. Often mistranslated as "law," this term in the Psalter refers to all of God's instruction, not just written texts like the Pentateuch). On Zion, God establishes the Davidic king, God's representative to Israel and to the nations (Ps. 2:6). The primary duty of humanity is to submit to God's rule (Ps. 5:2), to depend upon divine protection (Ps. 118:8–9), to meditate on *torah* (Ps. 1:1–2), and to follow the leadership of the Lord's anointed (Ps. 2:1–2). The righteous adhere to these characteristics (Ps. 37:39–40), and the wicked do not. The Psalms complain that the wicked oppress and prosper, but they also affirm a faith that, in the end, the wicked will fall (see Psalm 73).

> "The language of the psalms puts all who use them in the role of servants to the LORD God, and so lays a basis for an ethic of trust and obedience. It opens up a realm for existence in which the dying may take hope, the afflicted find strength, and the faithful encouragement." —James L. Mays, *The Lord Reigns: A Theological Handbook to the Psalms* (Louisville, Ky.: Westminster John Knox Press, 1994), 11.

Within this range of ideas, only briefly stated here, one perceives the Psalter's theology. The Psalms provide rich theological soil, so much so that Martin Luther called the Psalter "a little Bible." The heart of the theology of the whole Bible is contained in the Psalms, and much of Christian theology grows from the fertile ground of its poetry.

The Anatomy of a Psalm

What is a psalm? This question may seem so elementary as to need no answer or discussion. Isn't a psalm simply a poem found in the biblical book of Psalms? Yes, in a sense this is true, but the issue is much more complex than it appears at first. A quick look through the Bible reveals many poems of praise, lament, and thanksgiving which are outside the Psalter (e.g., Exodus 15; 1 Sam. 2:1–10; Luke 1:39–56). It is difficult, if not impossible, to show characteristics unique to the Psalms that distinguish them from other "psalms" in scripture. There are no common literary features to set the Psalms apart from other biblical poems. Yet the arrangement, order, groupings, or juxtaposition of the particular poems in the Psalter make statements about God and God's way in the world.

Given the prominence of psalms both inside and outside the Psalter, to answer the question "What is a psalm?" we must first understand the character, structure, and language found in any of the poems in the Bible, and then give particular attention to psalms in the Psalter. Psalm 3 is a good example for highlighting the features that define and help interpret the psalms.

> "The God one encounters in the Psalms is God as human beings have experienced him as both awake and asleep, gloriously present and lamentably absent, and above all, various." —Kathleen Norris, *The Psalms*, vii.

The Heading

The heading of Psalm 3 consists of the words "A Psalm of David, when he fled from his son Absalom." About two-thirds of the psalms in the Psalter have a heading. The heading functions like a title— it is not really part of the body of the psalm, and the rest of the psalms would make sense without it. For this reason, most translations place the heading in a different font or style of print, and do not include the words in the verses of the psalm. The headings are later additions to the body of the psalms that help direct how the psalm should be read or performed.

The heading in Psalm 3 has three main parts: (1) "Psalm" translates a Hebrew word *(mizmor)* that means "to praise God with music." So a psalm is usually defined as a "song of praise." (2) The phrase "of David" indicates that this song either was written for David, in honor of David, or was placed in a collection to commemorate that great king. (3) The final element of the heading of Psalm 3 is a biographical note explaining that this psalm was spoken by David as he fled from Absalom (2 Samuel 15). This tidbit provides an interesting insight into the history of the psalm. Since the headings were added later to the body of the work, the biographical note is not so much a historical report as a reflection on the character of David. Israel remembered David in an idealized way, much as Americans remember George Washington, Abraham Lincoln, and Martin Luther King, Jr. The best characteristics of these heroes sometimes become their only characteristics, or at least the only ones that are remembered. These heroes of a nation's past serve as models for what the country and its citizens ought to be. They inspire individuals to be better persons. Israel and, later, the church remember David as the model of piety who prays exemplary prayers, particularly in times of crisis (see the headings of Psalms 7; 18; 34; 51; 52; 54; 56; 57; 59; 60; 63; 142).

> "For Israel, this ascription did not necessarily indicate authorship, rather, it signified that the community identified itself with David as it came before God in worship."
> —Bernhard W. Anderson, *Out of the Depths,* 31.

The specific elements of the headings vary from psalm to psalm. Many of the titles include directions for the use of the psalm in worship, directions that are now obscure. For example, Psalm 7 is said to be a *shiggaion* of David. While the meaning of the label "psalm" *(mizmor)* on Psalm 3 is clear, the meaning of *shiggaion* is uncertain. Perhaps Psalm 7 was composed for a particular function in worship or somehow communicates a different type of message than other songs in the Psalter.

Some psalm titles include liturgical and performance directions—some that are clear (e.g., Psalm 30, "at the dedication of the

6

temple") and some not as clear (e.g., Psalm 22, "According to the Deer of the Dawn"). In addition to these notes concerning music and composition, most of the psalm headings attribute the psalm to someone: to David (Psalms 3–41; 51–71); to the Korahites (Psalms 42–49; 84; 85; 87; 88); to Asaph (Psalms 73–83); to Solomon (Psalm 72); to Moses (Psalm 90). As with the other historical references noted above, the names in the titles should not be understood to denote authorship in the modern sense. Rather, the names reflect traditions of Temple music (see 1 Chronicles 15–16), which remember David as the patron saint and others such as Asaph and the Korahites as prominent figures. The historical/biographical notes attached to thirteen psalms of David (including Psalm 3) are also extensions of this tradition.

Another strange term in the Psalms is *Selah*. This word is never part of a psalm title (it appears in the body of various psalms), but it may have some relation to the musical notations in the headings. *Selah* appears three times in Psalm 3 (vv. 2, 4, 8) and frequently in other psalms as well. Not enough is known about this word to give an exact definition, so English translations usually give the Hebrew word. In Psalm 3, *Selah* occurs at natural breaks in the psalm, as though marking paragraph divisions (but this is not the case in every psalm). Perhaps *Selah* was a musical or liturgical note whose significance has been lost. One plausible explanation for *Selah* is that the term might have been a signal to the Temple band, meaning something like, "Hit it!" Beyond that creative guess, little else can be said with certainty about the meaning of *Selah*.

Translation

An English-speaking reader depends on the work of others to understand the Psalter because the Psalms were composed in Hebrew. Any translation of biblical texts involves decisions about several matters. First scholars decide which ancient manuscripts of the Psalms are truest to the original wording of these poems. So, for example, the translators of the New Revised Standard Version provide a note to Psalm 3:2 to indicate their belief that the Syriac version ("there is no

> **PSALM 3.2**
>
> 2 many are saying to me,
>   "There is no help for you[b] in
>   God."   *Se′lah*
>
> *b* Syr: Heb *him*

Many translations offer an alternate reading.

help for *you*") is closer to the original than any of the available Hebrew manuscripts (which read, "there is no help for *him*").

Then scholars determine which English words are appropriate to render the original Hebrew words. In Psalm 3:2, the Hebrew word translated "deliverance" by the New International Version is rendered "help" by the New Revised Standard Version. A reading of several translations can show the possible range of meanings of many Hebrew words. No single translation always captures the sense of the Hebrew text in English, in part because the same English word has slightly different nuances of meaning for different people.

Poetry

The Psalms are poems, and poetry has distinct characteristics that merit special attention. In Hebrew poetry, two of these characteristics are rhythm and parallelism. The rhythm of the Hebrew language is hard to capture in an English translation. Verses 1–2 of Psalm 3 in the NRSV don't appear to have a rhythm, but the arrangement of the lines into stanzas of roughly equivalent lengths does communicate that a metrical pattern exists for reading, singing, or chanting this psalm.

Parallelism is more obvious in translations and, fortunately, is a more important characteristic of Hebrew poetry. Parallelism is the appearance of similar statements in two or three places. The similarities are not intended to be monotonous repetition. Rather, the parallel parts of the line complement, intensify, or advance the idea. For example, Psalm 3:1–2 contains an increasingly intense portrayal of the psalmist's enemies. The bare statement of their presence ("how many are my foes") in verse 1a takes on a more threatening tone as the psalm describes their activity ("many are rising against me") in verse 1b. First, the foes are identified as "many," but then the concept intensifies as those "many" become active and "are rising against me." Verse 2 goes further and records their taunt against the speaker: "There is no help for you in God."

Another type of parallelism appears in verse 4. This verse shows cause and effect: "I cry aloud to the LORD" (v. 4a); "and he answers me from his holy hill" (v. 4b). There are many types of parallelism, and once the reader is aware that parallelism may be present, discovering examples opens up a new appreciation for the creativity and depth of the Psalms.

The Psalms also communicate images through the use of simile, metaphor, idiom, and hyperbole. Psalm 3 is a good illustration. Verse 3 contains a metaphor: "But you, O LORD, are a shield around me." Unit 4, on Psalm 23, explores the nature of metaphor in more depth. Metaphors that the Psalms use to describe Yahweh include "rock," "fortress," "shepherd," and "warrior."

This picturesque language is indicative of poetry. Verse 7 contains idiomatic speech in the psalmist's declaration that Yahweh will "strike the cheek" and "break the teeth" of the enemy. The possible exaggeration of the number of enemies in verse 6 is an example of hyperbole. (The question as to whether "ten thousands" is intended as hyperbole or is a historical reference is difficult to answer. The Psalms do use hyperbole. However, so much of the language of the Psalter can be either literal or figurative, it is often difficult to decide which is the case. This difficulty is one of the challenges in psalm interpretation.)

 Want to Know More?

About translations of the Bible and ancient manuscripts? For a good understanding of textual criticism, see Richard N. Soulen, *Handbook of Biblical Criticism*, 2d ed. (Atlanta: John Knox Press, 1981), 192–96; also John H. Hayes and Carl R. Holladay, *Biblical Exegesis: A Beginner's Handbook*, (Atlanta: John Knox Press, 1987), 33–44. For the development of the scriptures, see John Barton, *How the Bible Came to Be* (Louisville, Ky.: Westminster John Knox Press, 1997), and *Holy Writings, Sacred Text: The Canon in Early Christianity* (Louisville, Ky.: Westminster John Knox Press, 1997). For a brief history of English translations, see Bruce M. Metzger and Roland E. Murphy, "English Versions of the Bible," in *The New Oxford Annotated Bible: New Revised Standard Version* (New York: Oxford University Press, 1991), 400–406.

About Hebrew poetry? See Metzger and Murphy, "Characteristics of Hebrew Poetry," in *New Oxford Annotated Bible* (NSRV), 392–97.

About Temple music? See Paul J. Achtemeier, ed., *Harper's Bible Dictionary* (San Francisco: Harper & Row, 1985), 667–71.

Body

Taking into account issues like translation and the poetic form of Psalms is helpful, but the main content or body of a psalm reveals the best indicators for interpretation. The body of Psalm 3 holds together as a unity. Any interpretation of this or any psalm must grapple with the nature of the body of the poem—its movement, coherence, and overall message. Analysis of the language and style reveals something of both the concerns the psalm communicates and the original function of the poem.

The style of Psalm 3 is dominated by direct address to God: "*O LORD,* how many are my foes!" (v. 1); "*You, O LORD,* are a shield around me" (v. 3); "Rise up, *O LORD!*" (v. 7). The frequent use of direct address marks Psalm 3 as a prayer (Mays, 6). In terms of the specific classifications introduced in the next unit, Psalm 3 is a "prayer for help of an individual." Verses 1–2 describe the trouble that requires Yahweh's action. The innumerable foes who taunt the psalmist are the chief dilemma. Verses 3–6 confess confidence in God's eventual delivery. This level of faith is typical of these prayers and serves as their foundation. Verse 7 repeats the pattern of petition/confidence. Then verse 8 praises the Lord and wishes for corporate blessing.

The exact occasion and the identity of the speaker of this prayer is impossible to determine. The references to a multitude of foes ("ten thousands of people"; v. 6) does not require a military setting, but does not rule out a military setting either. The language may be hyperbole or may reflect a genuine threat. The reference to Yahweh as a "shield" (v. 3) does not necessitate a battlefield scene; this is a common use of language and imagery. The difficulty of interpretation here is typical of the study of the Psalms.

Whether this is a real or figurative assault, an external military threat or a struggle within the psalmist, is not clear. Perhaps all that can be said is that the psalmist at the very least has a spirit troubled by the oppression of an enemy. The real threat may not be the enemy, but the temptation to believe that what the enemy says is true ("there is no help for you in God"; v. 2). Therein lies a temptation for every believer, that perhaps God is not in control or does not care or will not help. The psalmist defends against this temptation in verse 8, with the firm confession that "deliverance belongs to the LORD." This statement directly refutes the challenge of the enemy.

> " 'No salvation for him in God' is a mortally dangerous weapon against the soul. It has an ally in every crevice of doubt, anxiety, and guilt in the heart." —James L. Mays, *Psalms*, Interpretation, 52–53.

Context in the Psalter

The final consideration in interpretation is the placement of the psalm in the larger collection of poems. However, identifying the purpose in the arrangement of psalms in the Psalter is difficult, and in some cases, impossible. Not every psalm has a clear role to play in a larger message created by the whole, apart from being one of the general collection of material. But Psalm 3 is a different case. This work appears as the first psalm after the two introductory psalms (Psalms 1 and 2). Psalms 1 and 2 are held together by a shared vocabulary, including a wisdom formula ("Happy is . . .") at the beginning of Psalm 1 and at the end of Psalm 2. Psalm 2:12 concludes with the words, "Happy are all who take refuge in him." This language is a call to depend on Yahweh, to choose the protection of the divine king at all times. Psalm 3 follows this introduction with a prayer that models the kind of trust Psalm 2:12 elicits. Furthermore, in refuting the enemies' claim that "there is no help for you in God" (v. 2), Psalm 3 sets an example of faith that Psalms 1 and 2 indicate as essential for lifelong prosperity. The psalmist's confidence that "deliverance belongs to the LORD" (Ps. 3:8) proclaims a strength of faith that has taken refuge in the Lord. That is, we too should "take refuge" (Ps. 2:11) in ways illustrated by David (as indicated in the title), who cried to the Lord in the throes of life and depended on that same Lord for deliverance.

 ## Questions for Reflection

1. Too often the Bible is characterized as "ancient" and "irrelevant." The Psalms are a glowing example of how relevant the Bible can be. In this psalm, feelings like anxiety, trust, and confidence are discussed. What are some of the images for these feelings in Psalm 3? What are some things by which you feel threatened or that you are anxious about? What word of confidence does this psalm offer?

2. The title places this psalm in the events of the life of David, as described by 2 Samuel 15. Read that, particularly verse 30. How would you respond in that situation? What is David's example in this psalm?

3. *Selah* is used three times in this psalm. The explanation of its use as a signal for liturgical instruments to "Hit it" might conjure up the sounds of the brass and timpani from the theme of the movie *2001: A Space Odyssey*. Reread the psalm and note the rising intensity of the statements that follow *Selah*. How does this rereading affect your interpretation of the psalm?

4. Parallelism is one of the characteristics of poems like Psalm 3. For example, the word for "help" or "deliverance" (*yeshuʻah,* the word

from which the name of Jesus derives) appears throughout. What are other examples of parallelism? How does noticing these nuances help in the interpretation of this psalm?

Types of Psalms

Imagine the following scene: it is 11:00 A.M. on Sunday. The congregation gathers in the sanctuary. After the call to worship, everyone stands to sing. Confusion ensues because there is no hymn number in the bulletin, only these words: "It is now time to praise God. Choose words that will communicate a sense of adoration for who God is and what God has done." The worshiper might ask, "How? What words should I use? What has God done to prompt our praise?"

What would worship be like without hymns? Could worship even survive without hymns? Perhaps, but undoubtedly worship would have much less direction, form, and movement. Music plays an important role in worship. Like hymns in a modern church service, the Psalms were intended as lyrics for worship. Awareness of this intended use in worship is an important dimension is in understanding these poems.

> "Emotional immediacy, this ability to address people in all conditions of life, is what has made the Psalms the core of daily worship for both Jews and Christians for thousands of years." —Kathleen Norris, *The Psalms*, vii.

Knowledge about the Psalms in the Psalter and the experiences that lie behind them can help Christians learn to pray appropriately under diverse circumstances. This unit introduces the main types of psalms and their settings in Israel's worship.

The Importance of the Role of Psalms in Worship

Imagine two other worship scenes: in the first, a congregation gathers on Christmas morning and the choirmaster introduces the first hymn, "Jesus Walked This Lonesome Valley"; in the second, a congregation sings "Break Thou the Bread of Life" immediately before a baptism. In both of these situations, the worshipers would surely wonder what had gone awry in the planning of worship. In neither situation does the chosen hymn seem to correlate to its context in worship.

Just as many hymns are intended for use in particular times and events in the life of the church, many psalms were composed for certain times and seasons in the worship life of Israel. As in the singing of hymns, the appropriate recitation of psalms in worship events gave meaning to the Psalms. And the Psalms, in turn, contributed to the shape of those worship experiences. For many Christians, the hymn "Blest Be the Tie That Binds" is inextricably bound to the celebration of the Lord's Supper. The "tie" in the hymn represents the unity of believers that is experienced in Communion. In turn, that portion of worship for some people is not complete without "Blest Be the Tie." Put another way, Communion for many people has become the "context" in which that hymn makes sense. Such was the case with psalms and worship events in ancient Israel. One of the challenges in interpreting the Psalms is to discover the situation in Israel's worship that created the context for specific psalms.

The Use of Psalms

How were psalms used and on what occasions were they used? The study of the book of Psalms often begins by dividing the poems into groups that share the same literary form or "genre." The sorting of psalms in this way is called "form criticism," and it assumes that the literary form (genre) of a psalm reveals the intended setting in which the psalm was sung or chanted. The term "form" refers to both the type of language the psalm contains and its structure and movement.

"Christians have said them as their own prayers, as guides to learning to pray, and as texts through which they came to know themselves and God more surely."
—James L. Mays, *Psalms,* Interpretation, 2.

Does the psalm begin with a cry for help, an invitation to praise God, or a complaint? Is it spoken by an individual or a group? Does the psalm end in despair or hope? What problem(s) does the psalm seem to be describing? By asking questions like these, scholars classified psalms in different categories, with each category matching a different kind of worship experience. An understanding of these psalm classifications helps to determine the earliest use of the Psalms, and also has implications for their use in contemporary prayer and worship. Each of the psalm classifications reflects a distinct human response to God. A prayer at a funeral is different from a prayer at a child's birth because the experience and interaction with the Creator are different. Address to God is sometimes a cry for help, sometimes complaint, sometimes praise, and sometimes a call for justice.

The Prayer for Help of an Individual

The most common type of psalm is typically called an "individual lament." Actually Mays's label, "Prayer for Help of an Individual" (21) is more descriptive of the purpose of these psalms. Written in the first person, these psalms are characterized by a petition for God's help, an appeal to God to answer a prayer. An example is Psalm 7:1, which pleads,

> O LORD my God, in you I take refuge;
>> save me from all my pursuers,
>> and deliver me.

These psalms commonly describe a situation of trouble, usually in metaphorical language. Note, for example, the delineation of enemies in Psalm 22:12, 16 as "bulls" and "dogs." The requests for help often include a justification for the plea. The person praying begins with a declaration of innocence, freedom from guilt, and undeservedness of suffering. For example, Psalm 17 begins, "Hear a just cause, O LORD."

These prayers are grounded in trust and faith. In fact, more often than not they move sharply from complaint and petition to statements of confident assurance that indeed God will act and answer the prayer. Psalm 12 is typical of this movement, beginning with the desperate cry, "Help, O LORD, for there is

"The assumption behind all the prayers is that Yhwh's royal pleasure is found in the shalom of all who belong to his realm." — James L. Mays, *The Lord Reigns: A Theological Handbook to the Psalms* (Louisville, Ky.: Westminster John Knox Press, 1994), 28.

no longer anyone who is godly" (v. 1), but ending with the calm assurance, "You, O LORD, will protect us" (v. 7).

The original settings for these psalms are difficult to determine.

However, three situations often seem to be in view: (1) sickness, (2) accusation of a crime (the person praying is declaring his or her innocence), and (3) armed conflict (Mays, 22). Psalms 38, 26, and 3 respectively are examples of these three situations.

The Thanksgiving Song of an Individual

This category of psalm is partner to that of the prayer for help of an individual. The latter reflects a time of trouble from which a single worshiper asks deliverance; the former speaks of help that has already arrived for that person. These psalms praise God for divine deliverance, salvation, or response to the needs of the person praying. Psalms 30 and 116 are excellent examples. Although these psalms feature an individual voice, they are spoken much like a "testimony" in modern worship services. This is evident in Psalm 30:4, which moves from the testimony proper to encourage the congregation:

> "It is the joy of the one whom God has drawn up out of the dark depths, the joy of the one who has been freed from the 'bands of death,' the joy of the one in whose mouth God has placed a new song of praise to our God, of [the one] whose sorrow God has turned to joy." —Claus Westermann, *Praise and Lament in the Psalms* (Atlanta: John Knox Press, 1981), 112.

> Sing praises to the LORD, O you his faithful ones,
> and give thanks to his holy name

The individual "testifies" in a public way to what God has done. The thanksgiving song was possibly a public event in another way as well. The song likely accompanied a thanksgiving offering, as Psalm 116:17 indicates. These thanksgiving songs show the communal nature of worship in ancient Israel. Even recovery from illness was celebrated in a formal way in song and ceremony (Ps. 116:8–11).

The Corporate Prayer for Help

This type of psalm is the community's counterpart to the prayer for help of an individual. Rather than reflecting a personal need, these prayers arose when disaster struck the nation. With pleas for God to rescue, the corporate prayer urgently petitions God to hear and help. Psalm 80:1–2 begins,

> Give ear, O Shepherd of Israel,
>   you who lead Joseph like a flock!
> You who are enthroned upon the cherubim, shine forth
>   before Ephraim and Benjamin and Manasseh.
> Stir up your might,
>   and come to save us!

These psalms typically contain three elements: a description of the trouble (Ps. 79:1), an assertion of trust in the Lord (Ps. 74:12–17), and a recollection of God's saving deeds in the past. The last element is intended to "prime the pump" of God's salvation by making God's protection of Israel requisite to the claim that Yahweh indeed controls the universe. Psalm 74:23 states, "Do not forget the clamor of your foes," as if to say, "Lord, don't you want our enemies to believe in your power as we do? Rescue us!" Among the best examples of the corporate prayer for help are Psalms 44; 74; 79; 80; and 83.

> "The prayers are the voice of a community that knows that its last and best hope lies in the sovereignty of God." —James L. Mays, *Psalms*, Interpretation, 25.

The Hymn

In a sense, all the Psalms express praise. However, as Mays notes, "The function of praise in the Psalter belongs first of all to the hymn" (26). As the thanksgiving song is related to the prayer for help of an individual, so the hymn complements the corporate prayer for help. The hymns are relatively simple compositions. They typically have two elements: (1) an invitation to praise God; which is followed by (2) a statement of the motivation for praise.

The invitation is extended with a variety of expressions that call the community to lift up its voice in adoration of God. Sometimes the word *hallelujah* (Psalms 146–150) is used. This anglicized term is a combination of two Hebrew words, *hallelu*, an imperative meaning "praise," and *yah*, an abbreviated form of Yahweh, the personal name for God in the Old Testament (usually translated with the English term "Lord"). Another invitation to praise is, "Give thanks to the Lord" (Pss. 107:1; 118:1). Other expressions of the hymn's opening include, "O come, let us sing to the Lord" (Ps. 95:1), and "Make a joyful noise to the Lord, all the earth" (Ps. 100:1).

Psalm 95:1–3 illustrates well an invitation to praise that is followed by the second element, its motivation:

O come, let us sing to the LORD;
  let us make a joyful noise to the rock of our salvation!
Let us come into his presence with thanksgiving;
  let us make a joyful noise to him with songs of praise!
For the LORD is a great God,
  and a great King above all gods.

Little is known about the events that gave rise to the hymns of the Psalter except that the hymns were performed in Israel's yearly festivals (see Deut. 16:16–17). For examples of the hymn psalms, see Psalms 29; 47; 106; 107; 118.

The Psalms of Instruction

This group of psalms does not have recognizable characteristics in common like the categories of psalms described above. These psalms are united instead by their common interest in teaching a right way of life and a right way of worship. Their main goal is to encourage a righteous way of living (see Psalms 34; 37; 49) or teach the benefits of God's *torah* (see Psalms 1; 19; 119). These psalms were written in a time when teaching occurred through use of the language of prayer and praise. The "setting" of these psalms was not necessarily a "school" (Mays, 28). These psalms

God's law is more to be desired than gold. —Ps. 19:10

were used in worship, but they differ from other psalms because quite possibly they were written to instruct participants how to worship.

Since they lack a set of formal characteristics, psalms of instruction are hard to distinguish from other psalms. Nevertheless, several qualities characterize them. One is the use of the Hebrew alphabet to outline the psalm. These psalms, known as "acrostics," begin each line, or each section of the psalm, with a word that starts with the next letter of the Hebrew alphabet, until the whole alphabet is covered. Unfortunately, this acrostic is not apparent in an English translation. What is apparent, however, is that these psalms are intended to teach. Psalm 37:1–2 is an example of the "wisdom" themes in many acrostic psalms:

> Do not fret because of the wicked;
> do not be envious of wrongdoers,
> for they will soon fade like the grass,
> and wither like the green herb.

Additional examples of acrostics are Psalms 9–10; 25; 33; 111–112; 119; 145.

Some psalms of instruction contain beatitudes characterized by the expressions "blessed/happy/fortunate are those . . ." (the exact phrase depends upon the translation). Others seem to be a composite of different types of psalms (see Psalms 19; 33; 119), and still others serve as allusions to additional biblical passages (Psalms 103; 145). This last type of instruction psalms exhibits an awareness of "scripture." That is, these psalms presume a confidence in the inspiration and authority of certain texts. They "teach" by appealing to passages already known to the reader. A good example is the way Psalm 103:15–16 gives insight into the transience of humanity in ways similar to Isaiah 40:6–8:

Psalm 103:15–16	*Isaiah 40:6–8*
As for mortals, their days are like grass;	All people are grass, their constancy is like
they flourish like a flower of the field;	the flower of the field.
for the wind passes over it,	The grass withers, the flower fades, when the breath of the LORD
and it is gone;	blows upon it;
and its place knows it no more.	surely the people are grass.

Many of the psalms of instruction also emphasize topics like the benefits of *torah* (Psalms 1; 19; 119) or the final downfall of the wicked (Psalms 37; 49; 73).

Other Types of Psalms

These four categories do not exhaust the possibilities for categories of psalms. Indeed, many psalms fit none of these categories exactly. Some psalms revolve around the hopes of the Davidic king. These particular psalms celebrate his victories and lament his defeats

(Psalms 2; 45; 72; 89; 110). However, the four types of psalms listed above demonstrate the main ways Israel responded to God on specific occasions.

The Significance of the Psalm Categories

The categories and typical nature of psalm forms suggest that for the psalmists, worship had a conventional character. The same is true of prayer. Some Christians value prayers that are unique and unrehearsed. However, completely unique prayers are very rare. Most pray, and perhaps should pray, using language that comes from a well-known stock. That is not to say that address to God should be thoughtless, rote repetitions. The Psalms are certainly not so, even though they contain a common vocabulary. The stock phrases of the Psalms help a person pray with believers across the boundaries of time.

 Want to Know More?

About form criticism? See Richard N. Soulen, *Handbook of Biblical Criticism*, 2d ed. (Atlanta: John Knox Press, 1981), 71–74; John H. Hayes and Carl R. Holladay, *Biblical Exegesis: A Beginner's Handbook*, rev. ed. (Atlanta: John Knox Press, 1987), 83–91.

About how to used the Psalms in worship? See *Book of Common Worship* (Louisville, Ky.: Westminster John Knox Press, 1993), 1049–95; *The Psalter: Psalms and Canticles for Singing* (Louisville, Ky.: Westminster John Knox Press, 1993), 11–21; Elizabeth Achtemeier, *Preaching from the Old Testament* (Louisville, Ky.: Westminster John Knox Press, 1989), 137–63.

Learning to pray and offer praise with the traditional language of the church situates prayer in a communal context. This is particularly important for Christians in North America who live in a society that heavily emphasizes and values individualism. Christians should exercise faith not only in private but also in community. Some Christians also have biases against liturgy. Again, there are good and healthy aspects of worship that have spontaneity.

Yet one may miss the richness of the history of the faith if the traditionally accepted ways of expressing that faith are never experienced.

"The Psalms are not simply a record of God's encounters with people in the past, but a continual unfolding of God's revelation to us in the events of our ordinary lives." —Kathleen Norris, *The Psalms*, xxii.

Attention to the way psalms were written and the purposes for which they were written can enrich worship with an appreciation for time-tested, universally accepted forms of prayer, praise, and liturgical instruction. For many circumstances that might lead one to ask, "What words

20

should I use to pray?" or "What has God done to prompt our praise?" the categories of psalms presented here provide models for the answer.

 ## Questions for Reflection

1. What is similar and what is different about Psalms 11 and 12? What type of classification would you assign to each psalm? Why do you think these two psalms were placed together in the Psalter?
2. This unit emphasizes a way of studying the Psalms that is called the "form critical" approach because it highlights the fact that some psalms are so similar in form and content that they can be grouped together. Mays, however, cautions against using *only* this approach (20–21), because it can blur the distinct character of each individual psalm. Compare Psalms 30 and 116. Both are considered psalms of thanksgiving, and they have much in common. But they are also different in important ways. What are some of the differences?
3. The Psalms have contributed greatly to Christian worship and hymnody. What are some images of God found in hymns that are borrowed from the Psalms?
4. Psalm 37 is a psalm of instruction. What specific advice does this psalm offer? What is the continuing promise of the psalm? What is the relevance of that advice and promise today?

3 Psalm 1

The Way of the Righteous

As noted previously, Psalm 1 is not only the first psalm, but it introduces the entire Psalter. One reason we know that the Psalter was intended to be read and meditated on is the character of this first psalm. While most psalms are understood within the context of Israel's worship, Psalm 1 seems to be more for instruction and educational purposes. It reads like a passage out of the book of Proverbs. This difference in Psalm 1 suggests an intention about the composition and use of the Psalter. Placing first a psalm that is to be used outside the practice of worship indicates that the whole collection of Psalms was more than just some poems used for liturgy (though they never ceased to be that as well).

The Psalms presented material to be meditated and reflected on, writings that were thought to instruct the reader about God's will and how to follow it. The Psalms came to be seen not only as human words to God but also as God's word to humans. This understanding of the book of Psalms comes in large part from the character and position of the first psalm. Careful study of this psalm brings better understanding of the book of Psalms.

> "The Psalms serve as a good introduction to the Bible itself because they incorporate in poetic form so many of the themes of the Hebrew scriptures." —Kathleen Norris, *The Psalms*, xii.

Psalm as Beatitude

Psalm 1 may be called a "beatitude" because happiness is offered to those who abide by its statutes. The Hebrew term *ashre* begins the psalm and is commonly translated "blessed." This translation provides a link to the best-known beatitudes, those spoken by Jesus as recorded in Matthew 5:3–10 and Luke 6:20–22. However, the translation "blessed," both in Psalm 1 and in the Gospels, can be misleading. There was a practice in biblical times of bestowing a blessing. Through words and ritual, one granted favor to someone else, or "blessed them." The words of the blessing were thought to have magical power that provided prosperity. A good example of the significance of blessing is found in the story of Jacob and Esau (Genesis 27). The father, Isaac, spoke a blessing formula that apparently guaranteed his son Jacob success. When Esau realized that his brother had tricked both him and his father, he asked for a blessing too. To his chagrin, Isaac was unable to take back the blessing from Jacob, as if the words once spoken had a life and power all their own. What had been said was what must happen.

A beatitude, however, does not bestow or guarantee a blessed idyllic existence like the action of a magic genie. Instead, a beatitude describes what is already true for those who follow certain behavior. Granted, the "blessed" nature of life may only be recognized by those who discern the long-term joy of seeking and depending on God. That is precisely the point. A beatitude is an acknowledgment of the fortunes of those who submit to God's rule, fortunes that

> "They may not be great persons, as the world measures greatness, but they are blessed by a serene sense of the God-given meaning of life." —Bernhard W. Anderson, *Out of the Depths*, 222.

extend beyond present suffering and unhappiness. In other words, with a beatitude, good fortune is recognized as the natural outgrowth of life deemed "wise" by those who seek God's kingdom, not as a result of the words of Someone with power to "bless." So perhaps a better translation of *ashre* is "happy" or "fortunate."

Happiness Is . . .

What makes a person happy? Often in our modern world, happiness is tied to material possessions and "feeling good." Happiness for many is determined by owning the biggest and best or having pleasurable relationships. In the Psalter, however, "happiness" is something more permanent and stable that grows out of a dependence on God. Take for example the contrast of the righteous and wicked in Psalm 73. The writer contemplates the temptation to be envious of the wicked. The reason the psalmist desires the life of the wicked is simple: the wicked seem to have few worries; their bodies are strong, their wallets fat. When the psalmist comes into the presence of God, however, a glimpse of a future reality is given. The psalmist realizes that all the wicked have has been set in a slippery place (v. 18). A present-day analogy might depict the affluence of the wicked as a house built on sand, though it might seem strong and palatial in the present fair weather. To use another analogy, too often the wicked see life as a sprint, so success is defined by that which looks good in the present. In reality, life is more like a marathon. Only those with enough wisdom to run for the long term will be prosperous. When troubles come, the wicked fade and gasp for air, while the righteous pass by at a steady pace. It is this larger picture of life that the psalmist has in mind with the use of the term "happy."

Not the Wicked

The first picture of the happy person in Psalm 1 is given by counterexample: happiness describes those who are *not* like the wicked. Obviously this raises the question, Who are the wicked? Instead of identifying the characteristics of the wicked, Psalm 1 distinguishes them from the righteous. The wicked are called "sinners" and "scoffers" (v. 1). Mays states that the difference between the righteous and the wicked is derived from the "rightness or wrongness of one's response to the reality and revelation of the LORD's sovereign rule over human affairs" (43). The wicked are those who deny, as the hymn writer has said, that "God is the ruler yet."

The wicked appear in two prominent ways in the Psalter: (1) in the psalm type we call prayers for help of an individual, the wicked are those who afflict the righteous, accuse the innocent falsely of crimes, and give the righteous cause to question their trust in the Lord (Pss. 3:6–7; 10:2; 11:2); (2) in the corporate prayers for help psalms, the wicked threaten God's people and "put the course of the LORD's providence in question" (Mays, 43; Ps. 9:5–6, 17). Most of the time, the mention of the wicked provides a negative example of life; theirs is a life ultimately in conflict with the will of God (Ps. 5:4–6, 9–10). Note that the

"It is [God] . . . who secures the stability of [human] life; anything . . . which is done apart from God is bound to perish."
—Artur Weiser, *The Psalms*, Old Testament Library, 108.

24

wicked are characterized by independence, self-reliance, and overconfidence in their own abilities. For example, Psalm 49:6 describes the wicked as "those who trust in their wealth and boast of the abundance of their riches." The problem doesn't seem to be wealth or having ability. The problem is placing one's ultimate confidence in wealth or ability. The wicked are those who lose sight of their place as created beings, and arrogantly see the creature (i.e., themselves; see Rom. 1:18–32) as something more than it is. From this base of self-delusion, all manner of evil actions arise. Such a stance in life always leads to a fall, the psalmist asserts.

Delight in the Law

Use of the negative example as a foil for the righteous is not all Psalm 1 says about the nature of the "happy." Verse 2 moves to a more positive description:

> but their delight is in the *torah* of the LORD,
> and on his *torah* they meditate day and night.

Torah literally means "instruction." The word is quite often translated "law," and when capitalized in the Bible, the translators have in mind a written text like "books of Moses" (Genesis–Deuteronomy). This understanding of "Law" is too narrow for Psalm 1. Some of the Old Testament does use *torah* in this narrow sense, parts such as Deuteronomy and other closely associated writings (Josh.; Judges; 1 and 2 Samuel; 1 and 2 Kings). In those documents there is reference to "this *torah*" (see Joshua 1:8), calling to mind the legislation at the center of Deuteronomy. Psalm 1 does echo Joshua 1:7–8, so the psalmist is aware of *torah* as a written text (we would use the term "scripture"). Moreover, the fivefold organization of the Psalter seems to indicate a close association with the *Torah* in a narrow sense. However, *torah* as Psalm 1 uses the word is not limited to one document. *Torah* communicates the body of all instruction from God, in whatever form (a sermon, or even personal experience, to name two examples). The placement of Psalm 1 at the head of the Psalter, therefore, may mean that those who put the book together intend readers to receive *torah*

> "The LORD reaches, touches, and shapes the human soul through [*torah*]." —James L. Mays, *Psalms*, Interpretation, 42.

(divine instruction) from the psalms that follow. In time, the book of Psalms would become scripture, and would stand alongside the Pentateuch (Genesis–Deuteronomy) and the rest of the Old Testament as a written collection of God's revelation. One of the teaching points of Psalm 1 is that *attention to scripture and trust in scripture as a guide to life* are requisites for righteousness. The righteous who love and live *torah* will find their happiness there too.

> "Blessed are those who hear the word of God and obey it." (Luke 11:28)

Like Trees

After the statement that the righteous meditate on *torah*, Psalm 1 presents an extended simile to characterize the stability of the righteous (v. 3):

> And they shall be like trees
>   planted by streams of water,
> which yield their fruit in its season,
>   and their leaves do not wither.
> In all that they do, they prosper.

The simile of the green plant is common in ancient Near Eastern literature. In fact, the Old Testament uses this image several times (Jer. 17:5–8; Pss. 52:8; 92:12–13). The comparison of the righteous to an evergreen plant touches upon the perennial problem of why the righteous suffer and falter while the wicked flourish. Psalm 1:3 implicitly declares that in the long run, only faithfulness to the Lord, expressed in and made certain through devoted study of *torah*, makes one secure. The uses of this simile, however, perhaps need a bit more explanation.

"Like trees planted by streams of water"

In the two other places where the tree simile appears in the Psalter, the tree is planted in the Temple. In Psalm 52:8 the psalmist confesses:

> I am like a green olive tree
> in the house of God.
> I trust in the steadfast love of God
> forever and ever.

Similarly, Psalm 92:12–13 states:

> The righteous flourish like the palm tree,
> and grow like a cedar in Lebanon.
> They are planted in the house of the LORD;
> they flourish in the courts of our God.

This is a typical Old Testament way of speaking about the Temple. It is probably not so much historical as poetic. That is, this language comes from the idea that the Temple is a paradise. The Temple was for ancient Israelites a kind of "oasis for the soul." In the Temple, God's presence and power could be felt, the chaotic world made sense, and God's ultimate purpose for the world could be envisioned. The passages cited above imagine the righteous like one of the trees planted firmly before the throne of God. The righteous always have in their sights the will of God and God's rule over the world. Psalm 1:3 draws upon the trees-in-paradise image, and perhaps the trees-planted-in-temple image as well. As other evidence, the description of the tree in Psalm 1:3 is reminiscent of Ezekiel 47:12, another text that depicts trees planted around a paradiselike temple.

Two observations can be drawn from the simile of the righteous who are like trees planted in and around the Temple. Both rely on the assumption that Psalm 1 understands the stability that the righteous derive from meditation on *torah*. First, *torah* does for the believer what the Jerusalem Temple did: provides access to the presence of God, reveals the order of God's kingdom, and depicts the long-term wisdom of following the path of the righteous instead

Human hands cannot touch the scrolls, so the Torah is read always with the help of a pointing device known as a *yad*.

of the wicked. Second, since this psalm was probably written after the Jerusalem Temple was destroyed (in 587 B.C. by the Babylonians), the psalm may imply that *torah* has replaced the Temple. After the destruction of that holy place, the Temple was rebuilt (in 515 B.C.), but its vulnerability remained evident. Moreover, the Romans destroyed the rebuilt version in A.D. 70, and it was never reconstructed after that. After A.D. 70, Judaism indeed came to see *torah* as the supreme source of God's revelation. The people never forgot about the temple, and they continued to believe that there existed a perfect temple in the heavens (where God's throne rested). But now, through *torah*, one was able to gain access to God.

 Want to Know More?

About the practice of meditating on scripture? See Marjorie J. Thompson, *Soul Feast: An Invitation to the Christian Spiritual Life* (Louisville, Ky.: Westminster John Knox Press, 1995), 17–29.

About blessing and beatitudes? See Artur Weiser, *The Psalms*, Old Testament Library (Philadelphia: Westminster Press, 1962), 86–88; Eduard Schweizer, *The Good News according to Matthew* (Atlanta: John Knox Press, 1975), 80–82; also units 3 and 4 in Alyce M. McKenzie, *Matthew*, Interpretation Bible Studies (Louisville, Ky.: Geneva Press, 1998).

About the importance of the Temple to ancient Jews? See R. E. Clements, *Jeremiah*, Interpretation (Atlanta: John Knox Press, 1988), 43–45; for a thorough and technical discussion, see Horst Dietrich Preuss, *Old Testament Theology*, vol. 2, Old Testament Library (Louisville, Ky.: Westminster John Knox Press, 1996), 39–51.

About devotion to the Torah? See Rainer Albertz, *A History of Israelite Religion in the Old Testament Period*, vol. 2: *From the Exile to the Maccabees*, Old Testament Library (Louisville, Ky.: Westminster John Knox Press, 1994), 556–63.

Psalm 1 for Today

If these observations about *torah* in Psalm 1 are true, what are the implications for students of the Psalms, and students of scripture? Among other things, this psalm provides some guidance for reading and studying the Psalms. If the whole Psalter is to be understood as *torah* (as an essential part of scripture, which it certainly is), one should expect to find within this book testimony concerning God's election and salvation of Israel (as we find in Genesis–Deuteronomy), as well as a direction for living today. The contents of the book certainly provide both. Perhaps this is why Martin Luther called the book of Psalms a "little Bible." Reading and studying the Psalms closely will give a clear view of the "way of the righteous."

This psalm also says something of great importance about giving attention to scripture in general. Christians are "people of the book" in that they believe there is a written document (the Bible) that contains a record of God's will. One tragedy of today's religious life is that so little serious study of scripture is made. Not reading and meditating on scripture can be compared to starving to death while the cupboard is full of food! For Christians to live out their witness in the world, attention to scripture is essential. Without understanding scripture, their witness will be unfounded and go unnoticed. Moreover, as Psalm 1 states emphatically, learning the way of righteousness requires devotion to the source, and delighting in the contents. In a society that seeks instant gratification and emphasizes individualism as supreme, Christians would do well to learn from Psalm 1, and all the Psalms, about what can make a person "happy."

 ## Questions for Reflection

1. Who are the people you would call "blessed"? What are the characteristics of the blessed? Do you desire those characteristics (that is, would you like to be blessed)? Why or why not? What, if anything, can you do to be blessed?

2. Verse 2 refers to "delight" and the "law," two words not often joined together in today's understanding. One might delight in children or puppies, but usually the law is to be feared or obeyed. What does "delight in the law of the LORD" mean?

3. Verse 3 refers to trees whose "leaves do not wither"—evergreens, perhaps cedars. Find a good Bible dictionary and read the article on cedars. What does the image of an evergreen tree say about the righteous? The wicked are described as chaff. Read an article on chaff. What does the image of chaff say about the wicked?

4. Meditating goes in and out of fashion, and for some it conjures an image of navel gazing or the repetitious chanting of a phrase. The Hebrew word that is translated as "meditate" in verse 2 describes an ongoing sound, and has also been translated as "speaking" (Ps. 38:13), "growling" (as from a lion; Isa.31:4), "moaning" (in sorrow; Isa. 16:7), and even "musing" (Isa. 33:18). How does knowing this background of the word amplify your understanding of meditating on God's law?

4 Psalm 23

The Lord Is My Shepherd

On an episode of the old TV series *Gunsmoke,* an outlaw was traveling on a train, disguised as a minister. Doc Adams from Dodge City was on the same train, caring for a dying man. When death seemed imminent, the conductor sought the black-suited, clerical-collared outlaw to provide comfort for the man's final moments. Doc suspected the minister's true identity, but went along with the charade for the sake of the dying man. When the fake cleric reached the bedside, the injured man whispered, "The Twenty-third." The outlaw didn't understand, so Doc Adams prompted him, "He wants you to read the Twenty-third Psalm!" The imposter fumbled through the Bible he carried as part of his disguise until he at last located the psalm. He read the words awkwardly, as though for the first time. Even though an unfaithful voice offered the reading, the dying man was calmed. His favorite text soothed him as he passed into the shadow of death's dark valley.

> "Here is a poem that children have learned by heart, that has sustained the mature in the perplexities of life, and that has been a peaceful benediction on the lips of the dying." —Bernhard W. Anderson, *Out of the Depths,* 206.

This scene illustrates the power of scripture—the power to move, comfort, and guide the human heart in the extreme circumstances of life. This scene also typifies the popularity of Psalm 23. With a few possible exceptions, Psalm 23 is the most memorized and recited passage in the Bible. It is hard to imagine a funeral or an impending surgery where these familiar words are not quoted. Even the simple words "the Twenty-third" can identify this psalm.

A Guiding Metaphor

The psalm opens with a metaphor, "The LORD is my shepherd." A metaphor, like a simile, compares two things. A simile makes a comparison using "like" or "as": "*As* a deer longs for flowing streams, so my soul longs for you, O God" (Ps. 42:1). A metaphor is stronger and more direct than a simile, utilizing something that is commonly known to help describe something uncommon or unknown. The two things are not said to be merely like each other—a metaphor equates them: "The LORD *is* my shepherd." For this reason, a metaphor is a powerful figure of speech, but since it is a comparison, a metaphor should not be taken literally. However, it must be taken seriously.

"The LORD is my shepherd" is the guiding metaphor for the poem. This metaphor controls the poem, furnishes rich theological and spiritual depth, and almost certainly is the reason for this psalm's overall popularity. The rest of the psalm defines the benefits and privileges of being shepherded by God. Certainly Mays is correct when he says, "The psalm has been composed as the exposition of its opening line" (116). After the metaphorical statement, "The LORD is my shepherd," the psalmist adds the unqualified phrase "I shall not want." The absolute character of this second phrase is striking. Psalm 23 is an exposition of how the psalmist is completely fulfilled by the Shepherd.

The Shepherd as Metaphor

"Shepherd" is a vibrant, multilayered image that has many expressions in the Bible. On one level, a shepherd is someone who herds sheep. The sight of this activity and vocation was common for the ancients, and it is still seen in the Holy Land today. The shepherd guides the sheep to food and away from danger. As hired employees, shepherds in the ancient world were liable for the welfare of the sheep. If members of the flock were lost to ravenous beasts, shepherds had to account for their own efforts to defend against the predators (see the reference to the shepherds' responsibility in Amos 3:12). This picture of a shepherd's duties and responsibilities informs the line, "The LORD is my shepherd." Nevertheless, as Mays says, "the notion of being shepherd of persons opens up a background of tradition that is far broader than animal husbandry" (117). Metaphors as rich as this one typically expand beyond the level of common experience, so the shepherd metaphor is not limited to the vocation of caring for sheep.

> "The picture is one of the shepherd driving out the snakes from the pasture and clearing it of thorns before letting the sheep into it to graze. Then, when the sheep return to the fold at night, any cuts or bruises they have received are anointed with medicinal healing oil." —Elizabeth Achtemeier, *Preaching from the Old Testament* (Louisville, Ky.: Westminster John Knox Press, 1989), 141–42.

In the ancient world many types of leaders were called shepherds. This is particularly true of kings. Egyptian pharaohs are depicted often with a shepherd staff in hand or across the chest. It is no accident that tradition remembers David as a faithful shepherd. When David puts himself forward as the opponent of Goliath, he convinces Saul of his preparation for the fight by telling stories of how he defended sheep against bears and lions (1 Sam. 17:31–37). David's recollections present more than a résumé for a military post. Indeed, the story of his protection of the sheep is a symbolic affirmation of his suitability to be king.

That this metaphor had the vocation of shepherding in the background is obvious. However, the image is pliable enough to allow for development beyond sheepherding experiences. Ezekiel alters and expands the image to accuse Israel's shepherds (leaders) of "feeding on the sheep" (Ezck. 34:1–10). So what may never have been observed in the activity of real shepherds with sheep is introduced as part of a metaphor to describe the abuse of the populace by politicians.

The Divine Shepherd

The Old Testament associates God's shepherding with two defining experiences in Israel's corporate life: the exodus/wilderness (Pss. 77:20; 78:52–53; 80:1) and the exile (Isaiah 40:11; 49:9–10).

The former speaks of Yahweh's rescue and presentation to the promised land; the latter offers hope for a return to that land. The wilderness experience in particular echoes throughout Psalm 23. Mays points out the following connections with the wilderness accounts (118):

1. "I shall not want . . ." (which also could be translated, "I do not lack") recalls Deuteronomy 2:7, which states that during the forty years in the wilderness the Israelites "have lacked nothing."
2. "He leads me in the right paths" is similar to Exodus 15:13, which says God guided Israel to a holy habitation.
3. "You prepare a table before me" sounds much like Psalm 78:19, which declares that God can "prepare a table in the wilderness" for the people.

"My" Shepherd

Psalm 23 shares references with other parts of the Old Testament about God's provision, but the examples here highlight the larger context of the psalm's language. The shepherd metaphor, with all its varied expressions, raises the historical memory of a people shepherded by God. Unique to Psalm 23, however, is the extremely personal expression of God's care. Nowhere else in the Bible does anyone say, "the LORD is *my* shepherd." Herein lies the key to the vibrancy of Psalm 23 in the life of faith.

> "Perhaps in an indirect way the psalm prepares for the story of the shepherd who does leave the flock to go on a search for one lost sheep (Luke 15:4)." —James L. Mays, *Psalms,* Interpretation, 119.

This poem draws from a communal consciousness about God as a shepherd for the nation, but here the psalmist expresses this understanding in very personal terms. Many people in the ancient world believed in personal gods. Usually those individualistic expressions of relationship referred to a lesser deity in a pantheon. In Psalm 23, however, the psalmist declares that the Sovereign of the universe, the Creator of all things, can be described using "my," that the Lord attends to me in a personal way.

Psalm 23 as Lament

In the categories of psalms sketched in unit 2, "Types of Psalms," how would Psalm 23 be classified? Perhaps surprisingly, most scholars place this psalm under the general heading of individual lament or, as Mays says, prayer for help of an individual. Complaint psalms have faith and trust as their cornerstones. Those who are praying feel free to haul all their baggage to God because of their intimate relationship with the Lord. They are certain God will hear and answer. The complaint psalms move swiftly from plea for help and description of enemies to assurance that the Lord will deliver. Though Psalm 23 contains no complaint and is thoroughly a statement of trust, it still belongs to the category of lament. Behind the confession of faith in Psalm 23 are trials that required the psalmist to seek the shepherd's staff and tent for protection and shelter. All that we have of the psalmist's experience, however, is the beautiful poetic expression of confidence in the aftermath of threat and danger. That is, surely the psalmist experienced an unspecified threat, survived, and then composed this poem.

The entire psalm expounds the first line: "The LORD is my shepherd; I shall not want." The nature of what the psalmist does not want or lack comes to light as the poem develops. Verse 2 contains two pastoral images that go well with the shepherd metaphor: "He makes me lie down in green pastures; he leads me beside still waters." Both of these references emphasize tranquillity. The two words translated "green pastures" can also be translated as "beautiful new grass," a rarity in many parts of the Holy Land. "Still waters" could also be translated as "restful waters."

Verse 3a may seem startling: "He restores my soul (life)." These few words may mean that the psalmist was in physical danger, or they could refer to a revival, a rejuvenation in the general sense. The second understanding would complement verse 3b, which says, "he leads me in right paths." The implication may be that the shepherd puts the psalmist back on the right track in life, just as a literal shepherd directs the sheep.

A real danger seems implicit in verse 4, but the nature of the threat is far from clear. "Though I walk through the

---

Wherever he leads I'll go

In sunshine or through shadow, the faithful are "summoned to go with Yahweh into the future—like a flock that follows its shepherd into unexplored trails and new pastures." —Bernhard W. Anderson, *Out of the Depths*, 106.

---

darkest valley" has been interpreted as an allusion to a threat to the psalmist's life. The reference to "darkest valley" or "valley of the shadow of death" is no doubt why this text has become a standard at funerals. A single Hebrew word is translated as "shadow of death," but the word can also mean a valley that is "dark" and "shadowy." Whatever the exact meaning, the verse communicates a sense of danger. The ambiguity allows for application in many situations. Again, Psalm 23 is popular not just at funerals, but in all times of trouble or crisis.

Regardless of the threat, the psalmist is kept safe by the Lord's "rod and staff." A staff is easily understood as the crook of a shepherd, used to secure a sheep that might fall into a pit. Also the sick and elderly could find physical support from a staff (Ex. 21:19; Zech. 8:4). Singling out the reference to rod is more difficult. Perhaps the rod is a weapon for protection (2 Sam. 23:21; Micah 7:14) or a means to assemble and count the sheep (Lev. 27:32; Ezek. 20:37) or even the scepter of a ruler (Ps. 45:6; Amos 1:5; Zech. 10:11). Any of the possibilities still provide "comfort" to the psalmist, like that expressed in Isaiah 40:1, "Comfort, O comfort my people, says your God," another text that includes the shepherd metaphor (see Isa. 40:11). Again here, however, Psalm 23 claims that comfort in a most personal way.

The Divine Host

A close reading of verse 5, placed in the ancient Near Eastern context, reveals a second metaphor in the psalm. Verse 5 depicts God as host:

> You prepare a table before me
>   in the presence of my enemies;
> you anoint my head with oil;
>   my cup overflows.

In the background here is an ancient tradition of hospitality. The Lord is a host who gives refuge to one beset by enemies. When inside the protective shelter of the host's dwelling, the psalmist is offered abundant food and drink, oil for grooming, as well as the assurance of safety. What was communicated in verses 1–4 in the use of the shepherd metaphor is paralleled here in the use of a host metaphor. This point is essential to grasp the fullness and complexity of Psalm 23. However, the meshing of two metaphors in no way suggests that the poem is disjointed. The psalmist utilizes the hospitality imagery so adeptly as to make an almost seamless transition. And

though a second metaphor is employed, the shepherd metaphor legitimately can still be said to define and control the picture of God in Psalm 23.

The images of host and shepherd find common ground in the place of God's shepherding and sheltering— the Temple. The Temple of the Lord provides both the primary pasture for God's sheep and the ultimate refuge for those under the protection of the divine host (Pss.

"You prepare a table before me"

36:7–9; 95:6–7; 100:3–4). Therefore, that the two metaphors merge comes as no surprise. As noted already, the image of human shepherding does not convey adequately the full notion of God as shepherd. The portrait of God as host helps fill out the shepherd metaphor, expanding the range of meaning and adding to the variety of ways God can serve as shepherd.

Goodness and Mercy

"The shepherd can be portrayed from two standpoints. He is the protector of the sheep as they wander in search of grazing land. Yet he is also the protector of the traveler who finds hospitality in his tent from the dangers and enemies of the desert." — Bernhard W. Anderson, *Out of the Depths*, 208.

Psalm 23:6 concludes with two of the most hopeful claims in scripture. The first hope is that "Surely goodness and loving-kindness shall pursue me all the days of my life" (v. 6a; Mays's translation). That "goodness" will follow the psalmist probably needs no explanation. The second term, "loving-kindness," however, is more complex.

"Loving-kindness" translates the Hebrew word *hesed*, which is used of Yahweh's covenant faithfulness. *Hesed* is one of those words that is so pregnant with meaning as to allow for translation with several

English terms. Perhaps "faithful" could be added to Mays's rendering, "loving-kindness," but even so, Mays's translation is better than "mercy," as found in many English versions. The psalmist is claiming that the way of Yahweh, as illustrated by Yahweh's faithful rescue of the Israelites from Egypt, providing guidance in the wilderness, and helping them possess the promised land, will be the way of Yahweh with the psalmist.

> "Steadfast love is both character and act. One can attempt to define it as helpfulness toward those with whom one stands in relationship. To do *hesed* is to do the best in and make the best of a relationship." — James L. Mays, *Psalms,* Interpretation, 328.

The psalmist's second hope is that "I shall dwell in the house of the LORD my whole life long" (v. 6b). The house of the Lord is the Jerusalem Temple. Only the priests and Levites, who came in shifts to work for part of the year, would literally live in the Temple. Therefore, Mays questions whether there might be an institutional setting for this psalm (116). That is, perhaps this psalm was composed for liturgical use in the Temple by those who lived there. An exact explanation cannot be determined, but Mays's question still raises important issues about the composition and intent of the Psalms. Psalm 23 might have been composed by a professional poet, one of the Levites who served as a Temple musician (see 1 Chronicles 15–16). Perhaps the author was one who held the Temple so dear, he imagined it as the supreme location of God's presence, a place where "goodness and loving-kindness" could be experienced most completely. If so, then the psalmist was saying that the food that grows in the paradise of God's presence provides the pasture for God's sheep.

 Want to Know More?

About shepherds in biblical times? See Madeline S. Miller and J. Lane Miller, *Harper's Encyclopedia of Bible Life,* 3d rev. ed. (New York: Harper & Row, 1978), 141–44.

About the role of a host? See both Paul J. Achtemeier, ed., *Harper's Bible Dictionary* (San Francisco: Harper & Row, 1985), 408–9, and George Arthur Buttrick, ed., *The Interpreter's Dictionary of the Bible,* vol. 2 (Nashville: Abingdon Press, 1962), 654; see also Marjorie J. Thompson, *Soul Feast: An Invitation to the Christian Spiritual Life* (Louisville, Ky.: Westminster John Knox Press, 1995), 120–21.

About loving-kindness (hesed)? See James L. Mays, *Psalms,* Interpretation (Louisville, Ky.: John Knox Press, 1994), 33, 326–31, 418–21.

Jesus, the Best Shepherd

The shepherd image appears not only as part of the Old Testament but as a vital part of the New Testament as well. For Christians, Psalm 23 foretells the words of Jesus, "I am the good shepherd" (John 10:11), and the writer of 1 Peter who declares that Jesus is the "shepherd and guardian" of souls who leads believers when they are "going astray like sheep" (2:25). Jesus is indeed the "chief shepherd" (1 Peter 5:4) for the church. As Mays appropriately notes (119), seeing Jesus as the supreme shepherd calls Christians to look to God's guidance for the future, as well as the present. In the age to come, the Lamb of God will become king and shepherd, and in that day, the redeemed will discover in their hearts the full meaning of the phrase, "I shall not want" (see Rev. 7:15–17).

 ## Questions for Reflection

1. Shepherd is the guiding metaphor for this psalm. In what ways is God like a shepherd? What are other metaphors for God?

2. In an age where the media bombards us with pictures of things we should want, how realistic is the claim of verse 1, "I shall not want"? What does the phrase mean?

3. Churches, companies, and countries are desperately in need of good leadership. If Psalm 23 provides a model for leadership, what are the characteristics of a good leader?

4. There is a Hebrew word for "follow" which has the sense of "to walk" (Ps. 1:1). Here, though, the word has the sense of "pursue." Psalm 23:6 could be translated, "Surely goodness and God's covenant love will *pursue* me all the days of my life." How does this translation affect your interpretation and application of the psalm?

5

"I Have Sinned against You"

The scene is repeated countless times in nameless dramas and forgettable made-for-TV movies. After a series of ill-conceived choices, followed by an outbreak of dysfunctional behaviors in a family, a child comes to a parent, and with great remorse confesses, "I am so sorry: I ruined my whole life, and made a mess out of everything." And, as if possessing the wisdom of the ages, the parent comfortingly responds, "There, there, you haven't ruined your whole life—only your summer vacation."

Though the illustration makes light of it, the statement, "I am so sorry: I ruined my whole life," is a serious statement, and also one of penitence. Penitence is an integral part of Christian life and prayer. Many believers are introduced to the life of meditation along the path of the Lord's Prayer, which includes the words, "forgive us our debts, as we forgive our debtors." Most learn the story of the prodigal son (Luke 15:11–32) as a model of relationship between God and believer. Worship services typically include a formal time for the confession of sins. In light of the prominence of penitence, a

Return of the Prodigal Son
Etching by Rembrandt Harmensz van Rijn, 1636.
Fine Arts Museums of San Francisco.

novice reader of the psalms might be surprised to learn that only a few psalms of this type are in the Psalter. Most of the prayer psalms cry for help or complain about the prosperity of the wicked (and even argue for the innocence of the psalmist!). Only seven psalms stand out as "penitential" (Psalms 6; 32; 38; 51; 102; 130; 143), and some of these contain little one would recognize as penitence.

Psalm 51 is an exception. The sharpest and most complete expression of the penitential theme is present here. Traditionally Psalm 51 is used to introduce the season of Lent, and for that reason it has exercised an enormous influence on the church's theology and liturgy. This psalm also has shaped the prayers of individual Christians, both privately and publicly, as much or more than any other single psalm.

A Prayer for Help

Prayers of repentance do not have a reserved place in the categories of psalms discussed in unit 2. Psalm 51 belongs to the larger classification of prayers for help, though obviously the psalmist's trouble arises from a sinful state. The opening line (v. 1a) pleas, "Have mercy on me, O God, according to your steadfast love (*hesed*)," and the remainder of the psalm expounds on both the request for help and the assumption that the Lord is merciful.

> ### What Wondrous Love Is This?
>
> The psalmist throws himself upon the mercies of God by appealing to two very powerful images of love: God's steadfast covenant love *(hesed)*, and the womb imagery of a mother's love. —George A. F. Knight, *Psalms*, Daily Study Bible, vol. 1 (Philadelphia: Westminster Press, 1982), 241.

The superscription indicates a well-known setting in the life of David. David has had an affair with Bathsheba; her husband, Uriah the Hittite, has been killed in battle; and the prophet Nathan has confronted David with his wrongdoing. The psalm's title pitches the work as David's prayer after the meeting with Nathan. Like the other superscriptions that place psalms in the life of David, the title of Psalm 51 is motivated by several parallels of language between the psalm and the story (2 Sam. 12:1–23). The psalm's opening wish, which could be translated as "Be gracious to me" (Ps. 51:1), sounds like 2 Samuel 12:22; the confession, "Against you, you alone, have I sinned," is similar to David's confession in 2 Samuel 12:13; ". . . and done what is evil in your sight" (Ps. 51:4b) is nearly identical to the evaluation of David's deed in 2 Samuel 11:27, which reads literally, "what David did was evil in the eyes of the LORD"; the psalmist's request to be delivered from bloodshed (Ps. 51:14) fits nicely with the whole story of David sending Uriah into battle to be killed (2 Sam. 11:14–25).

The connection between Psalm 51 and David's treachery (like Psalm 3; see unit 1) probably results from the work of a scribe who knew his Bible like the back of his hand. The intent was to provide a model of repentance by setting this psalm in the context of David's life. That is, upon recognizing personal sin, one should behave like David, fall before God in sorrow, and make a request in the manner of Psalm 51 for deliverance from evil. Unlike the frivolous presentation by the TV program, for most of us the evil is more severe than a messed-up summer vacation. Like the prodigal's words at his return to his father (Luke 15:21), David's example instructs believers in forming personal prayers of confession.

> Confessing your sins doesn't tell God anything new. In the words of Frederick Buechner, "Until you confess them, however, they are the abyss between you. When you confess them, they become the bridge."
> —*Wishful Thinking*, 15.

A Prayer for the Community

One of the most important uses of this psalm in the church has been in corporate prayer. There are elements of the psalm that suggest the work was prayed in a communal setting in ancient Israel as well. Perhaps the best illustration of this is verses 18–19:

> Do good to Zion in your good pleasure;
>   rebuild the walls of Jerusalem,
> then you will delight in right sacrifices,
>   in burnt offerings and whole burnt offerings;
>   then bulls will be offered on your altar.

These words assume the devastation of Jerusalem and the destruction of the Temple in 587 B.C. by King Nebuchadnezzar and the Babylonians. Some portions of Psalm 51 read like the later parts of the prophetic books of Ezekiel, Jeremiah, and Isaiah that offer hope for the restoration of Jerusalem. The words of Psalm 51:10 sound like Jeremiah 24:7; 31:33; 32:39–40; or Ezekiel 36:25–26, which all speak of a new heart given by God to faithless Israel. The Ezekiel text in particular emphasizes God's cleansing that will produce this new heart. Psalm 51 magnificently expresses the idea that the ritual of sacrifice should arise from a pure heart and a penitent spirit.

With such an emphasis, Psalm 51, and the prophetic texts mentioned, give counterexample to the commonly held opinion that the Old Testament advocates empty ceremony while the New Testament promotes grace through faith. Few texts in the New Testament state more clearly the notion that one must depend on God's free gift of salvation (his "graciousness"; v. 1); few texts in the New Testament say with as much clarity that outward expressions of devotion to God necessarily come as witness to what has occurred within the heart. Psalm 51 insists that the nation, as well as the individual, exercise purity in worship.

> **Did You Know?**
>
> There is no developed concept of a trinitarian God in the Old Testament. Here, in Psalm 51:11, and in Isaiah 63:10–11 are the only places the words "holy spirit" appear in the Old Testament.

A Prayer of Petitions

As Mays observes about Psalm 51, "petitions are in control of the structure throughout" (198). Verses 1–2 contain four requests: "have mercy"; "blot out my transgressions"; "wash me"; "cleanse me." This petition for purification is picturesque, particularly the request "wash me." The Hebrew word refers to a cleansing by beating, treading, and kneading. It is a laundry term. The picture of purification moves in progression from outside to inside: blot out (like outwardly wiping a dish); wash (launder); and cleanse (purifying the inner self).

"Wash me"

In a similar fashion, the terms for wrongdoing pile upon each other. They accumulate to make an all-encompassing statement about what is cleansed: rebellion (translated "transgressions");

shameful acts ("iniquity," that which causes guilt); and mistakes ("sin," literally: "missing the mark"). The poetry here communicates the severity of the psalmist's disobedience and the intensity of the desire not only for forgiveness but also for purification from sin and the effects of sin.

Verses 3–6 contain only one petition (v. 6b), but this section supports the previous requests with a recognition of guilt: "I know my transgressions, and my sin is ever before me" (v. 3). The awareness of sin produces the realization that God's sentence is justified. The statement, "against you, you alone, I have sinned," is often misunderstood as a denial of sin's consequences for other persons. In the story of David and Bathsheba, David declares, "I have sinned against the LORD," after being confronted with his crime. That line, as well as verse 4a of the psalm, must be read in the context of God's judgment. Sin is said to be "against the LORD" because God is the one who calls a sinner into judgment. However, all sinful acts affect others. This text indicates that accountability for sin is a larger issue, and the bigger context of God's judgment increases the weightiness of the whole matter.

> "The trouble is wholly the sinful self." —James L. Mays, *Psalms*, Interpretation, 198.

Verse 5 summarizes this section and completes the statement of the psalmist's sinfulness. This verse can be misread as a record of illegitimate birth or as a denunciation of human procreation in general. A more accurate view recognizes the writer's use of typical poetic devices to intensify the confession of guilt. As Mays points out (201), numerous Old Testament passages use birth imagery to describe the nation's rebelliousness (Isa. 48:8; 50:1; Ezekiel 16; 20; 23). The writer of Psalm 51:5 may have these in mind, but the statement here is voiced by an individual. Moreover, the psalm presents a self-condemnatory line, unlike the prophetic texts.

The psalmist offers a reverse narrative that describes the birth process, from birth itself back to conception. Verse 5 heightens the magnitude of the writer's sense of sinfulness, as if the psalmist says, "I am such a horrible sinner that I was sinful at birth" (v. 5a), and then, dissatisfied with that expression, follows with, "No, that's not strong enough. I was sinful long before birth—I was a sinner even at conception!" (v. 5b). Remember that this is poetry, poetry that relies on parallelism to make a point. Being poetry, the line is not meant to be taken literally or to be read as a systematic theology about the origin of sin or depravity of the human condition. Instead, allow the intensity and movement of the poetic line (from birth to conception) to cast light on the depths of human sinfulness. Humans do not just perform sinful acts; they *are* sinful creatures. Humanity is part of a corrupted universe, and human imperfection does not begin with the first act of rebellion. To share this recognition with the psalmist makes possible the shared awareness that only God can blot out, wash, and purify the human spirit. In all confessions of sin, whether corporate or private, the two extremes of human unfaithfulness and God's healing power are held in tension. Psalm 51:1–6 is an ideal text to help us wrestle with this theological and spiritual tension.

A Prayer for Renewal

Verses 7–12 continue with petitions for forgiveness and cleansing from sin, but with an added emphasis on renewal. Prayers of penitence can become meaningless rituals that make no difference in how life is lived. There are times when the corporate prayer of confession in Sunday morning worship may seem so: the congregation recites a prayer acknowledging sins, and the minister declares repetitively, "In Jesus Christ, you are forgiven." If this procedure feels routine, like an exercise in cheap grace, consider the words of Psalm 51:7–12. This section of the psalm reminds Christians that a relationship with God is of the character of the closest human encounters. When one disobeys a parent, or does something to harm one's spouse, the words "I'm sorry" are simply not enough. There must be some restoration of trust and closeness, and some revitalization of the relationship. Like the prodigal who "came to himself" (Luke 15:17) and in his confession of sin "against heaven and before you" (15:21) asked to live only as the father's servant, so repentance must be accompanied with real change. For the psalmist, the request for renewal is both as important as, and the logical outcome of, the acknowledgment of transgressions.

"Pastors can be so reluctant to use the word 'sin' that in church we end up confessing nothing except our highly developed capacity for denial. One week, for example, the confession began, 'Our communication with Jesus tends to be too infrequent to experience the transformation in our lives You want us to have.' . . . At such times I picture God . . . who leans across a table and says, not at all gently, 'Could you possibly be troubled to say what you mean?' It would be refreshing to answer, simply, 'I have sinned.' " —Kathleen Norris, *Amazing Grace: A Vocabulary of Faith* (New York: Riverhead Books, 1998),

44

The request is for a "clean heart," a "new and right spirit" (v. 10), and restored joy (v. 12a). An important part of these requests is the verb "create" in verse 10. The Hebrew word is *bara*, a term usually reserved for God in the Old Testament (Mays, 202). For example, *bara* is used in Genesis 1:1 to describe the ordering of the universe. So when the psalm turns to the theme of renewal, it is not merely a promise of self-help. Indeed, the psalmist recognizes once again a need for reliance on the Lord. God alone can "create a clean heart" (v. 10a) and establish "a right spirit" (v. 10b). Presumably the psalmist means a spirit

> "The Hebrew word for 'heart,' which is here parallel to 'spirit,' does not refer to the seat of emotions as in English (in Hebrew that would be 'kidneys' or 'bowels'). Rather, 'heart' refers to the mind and the will, that is, the center of the self from which action and loyalty spring." —Bernhard W. Anderson, *Out of the Depths*, 97.

that is open to God's will, and a heart that trusts in the Lord in difficult times (see Ps. 112:7–8). The requests for renewal at numerous points echo language of Israel's experience in exile: references to "joy" and "gladness" sound much like the prophetic and psalmic descriptions of Israel's jubilation at the return from exile or exodus (Ps. 105:43; Isa. 55:12). Just as God initiated and carried through those experiences of deliverance, so the Lord must restore the sinful heart.

The Sacrifice of a Broken Spirit

The psalm concludes with a mixture of references to (1) proper sacrifices, (2) hearts turned toward God, and (3) rebuilding Jerusalem's walls. In this psalm, these three topics are interrelated and almost inseparable. Only sacrificial rituals from those with "broken spirits" will be accepted. By "broken spirit," the psalmist does not mean someone who is lifeless or without determination. Rather, this description implies a spirit that is turned over to God's control: one who is not arrogantly self-reliant. Again, the image of the prodigal's return in his humble stance before the father captures the essence of the "broken spirit." This idea is the key to understanding this psalm. "The psalm itself is the liturgy of the broken heart" (Mays, 203). Note, however, that the psalm does not say sacrifice is prohibited or unwanted. Rather, the psalm puts sacrifice in proper relationship to righteousness; the former being the natural expression of the latter. This characteristic of the psalm shows the influence of prophetic ideas like those in Amos 5:21–24 and Micah 6:6–8. These voices are apparent throughout the psalm. The psalm's references to being purified and cleansed are like the prophetic references to inward purity that produces justice.

The idea of rebuilding Jerusalem may not seem as clearly connected to right spirit as is the idea of proper sacrifices, but the relationship becomes apparent upon closer examination. The restoration of Jerusalem represents God's renewal of the nation. The restored walls of the holy city are evidence of the people's hearts now restored to right relationship with the Lord. When both of these elements of restoration are made, sacrifices will again be properly established. This connection between the nation and repentance suggests the communal nature of this psalm and of penitence. As people make individual confessions of sin, they do so as part of a larger community of faith, whose fate and mission are bound together.

Want to Know More?

About biblical understandings of seeking forgiveness and atonement? See Paul J. Achtemeier, ed., *Harper's Bible Dictionary* (San Francisco: Harper & Row 1985), 80, 1143–47.

About contemporary approaches to prayers of confession? See Marjorie J. Thompson, *Soul Feast: An Invitation to the Christian Spiritual Life* (Louisville, Ky.: Westminster John Knox Press, 1995), 83–99.

About traditions of penance? See Richard P. McBrien, ed., *The HarperCollins Encyclopedia of Catholicism* (San Francisco: HarperSanFrancisco, 1995), 982–83.

Corporate confession is appropriate because of the communal nature of sin itself. Sin is not so much an act as a state of being common to all of us. The consequences of individual sin reach beyond the sinner alone. The whole community is affected. Trying to isolate sin to one individual is like trying to characterize a life's worth of mess up as merely a ruined summer vacation. The whole community is affected; the whole community needs to make amends. Psalm 51 expresses the depths of this truth and offers a beautiful vocabulary with which to seek peace with God.

? Questions for Reflection

1. In Mays's words (198), there is an "unrelieved intensity" about this psalm, and particularly in the first line. What are some feelings you connect to an "unrelieved intensity"? How does this psalm speak to those feelings?
2. Only two crimes in Old Testament times could not be atoned for

by sacrifices: rape and murder. If the setting for this psalm is correct, David has commited both. Without atonement, David cannot have a relationship with God. In the modern idiom, he has been excommunicated (he can't come to church anymore). What requests, then, does David make in this psalm?

3. The story of David's sin, and the requests of this psalm involve the tension between human failure and divine grace. What are the claims of Psalm 51 about this tension?

4. Psalm 51 suggests that every sin is a sin against God. Why is this so?

6 Psalm 99

Rejoice, the Lord Is King

A couple returned home one night to their four-year-old daughter who was in the care of a teenage babysitter. It was close to Valentine's Day, and the daughter and sitter had produced several pieces of artwork with a Valentine theme. The babysitter's contribution to this project included a series of hearts around the statement, "Hanson rules!" Hanson is a popular music group that appeals to adolescent girls, so her admiration for the group was not surprising.

The common parlance of youth today is to declare that someone or thing they admire "rules." This line is a bold and honest statement of loyalty to a particular person or idea. To say that someone rules evokes the language of monarchy. Though a youth may not intend to do so, such a statement reminds us that we all are controlled by various forces in the world, whether consciously or not. As youth and adults struggle with where to assign loyalty and devotion, the Psalter offers direction with its own take on the rulership issue. The Psalms declare, "The LORD rules (or reigns)."

Praising God the King

Psalm 99 is one of many psalms to use "The LORD reigns" as a controlling idea. This declaration is *the* central claim about God in the Psalter, and the concept of the "kingdom of God" is central to all biblical faith.

Though it does not follow the exact description given in "Types of Psalms" (unit 2), Psalm 99 is nonetheless a hymn. Instead of beginning with an invitation to praise, this psalm opens with the declaration, "The LORD reigns." (The NRSV reads, "The LORD is king." The Hebrew term *malak* allows translations that describe God in terms of activity [he rules] or office [he is king].) This change in the conventional beginning of the hymn identifies this psalm as a special type of hymn called an "enthronement psalm." Other enthronement psalms include Psalms 47; 93; and 95–99. These works are united by their common praise of God as king, as one "enthroned." Many of the comments about Psalm 99, then, hold true for all the psalms in this group.

> The Hebrew word for king *(melek)* is found in this often-used Jewish mealtime blessing:
>
> Barukh ata Adonai, Eloheinu **melekh** ha-olam ha-motzi lechem min ha-aretz. (Blessed are you, Lord our God, King of the universe, who brings forth bread from the earth.)

"The LORD reigns" and the words that follow call the subjects of the heavenly king to stand in awe before God. Behind this declaration is a rich idea held by ancient Near Eastern peoples that a deity was a cosmic monarch. For Israel's neighbors, this belief reflected the human political situation fairly accurately. In their understanding, just as earthly leaders struggled to get to the top of the heap, gods vied for control of the cosmos, and the most powerful among them was named king. By contrast, Israel thought of Yahweh as the absolute ruler, having no rivals—past, present, or future.

God Is a Many Splendored King

Israel shared with other ancient Near Eastern people the belief in a multifaceted role for the divine king. Under the umbrella concept of king, many of the metaphors for Yahweh in the Psalter can be understood. For example, that Yahweh is king means that Yahweh is creator, the one who rules over chaos. For ancient people, chaos was symbolized by the unruly force of water; therefore, much of God's activity in creation dealt with taming and delimiting the seas. We see this in Psalm 93:4, which says,

> More majestic than the thunders of mighty waters,
>   more majestic than the waves of the sea,
>   majestic on high is the LORD!

The Lord rules over the chaotic waters, and that control is an important mark of divine kingship.

The image of God as king also supports a series of other

metaphors that can be grouped under the heading "protector." Among these images are shepherd, refuge, warrior, and judge. The label "warrior" might be offensive to some when applied to God because many only see God as a loving and forgiving parent. Also, warlike metaphors may seem out of place in a faith that includes Jesus' teachings to "turn the other cheek" and "love your enemies." Some tension exists in these various biblical portraits of the divine. However, we cannot simply remove the images that cause discomfort. Furthermore, the warrior image is a constant in the Bible, including the New Testament (Rev. 17:14; see also references to the Christian life as a war/battle: 2 Cor. 10:3–4; Eph. 6:11–17; 1 Tim. 1:18; 2 Tim. 2:3–4; James 4:1–2; 1 Peter 2:11).

"The LORD is a warrior"

When the Lord rescued the Israelites from the Egyptians, God's people proclaimed, "The LORD is a warrior" (Ex. 15:3), and declared that "the LORD will reign" (15:18). Psalm 98:1b–2 likewise states:

> His right hand and his holy arm
>   have gotten him victory.
> The LORD has made known his victory;
>   he has revealed his vindication in the sight of the nations.

These two references tell us that God is a warrior who defends the people with vigor against their enemies. Again, this idea may not satisfy modern notions of peacemaking, but it is perfectly consistent with the ancient Near Eastern expectations of kings. Monarchs were responsible for defending their people, and their ability to do so was a measure by which their success was judged. Faith today must be worked out in a world very different from that which produced the enthronement psalms; a discussion of the appropriateness of the kingship model for the shape of contemporary faith comes later in this unit. For the moment, however, suffice it to say that the presentation of the Lord as a warrior in some of these psalms (and other places in the Old Testament) helps create a picture of God as the ideal king.

The Lord Is in His Holy Temple

Psalm 99 falls naturally into three parts: verses 1–3; 4–5; 6–9. The divisions are marked by the words "Holy is he," which recur as a refrain at the end of verses 3 and 5 (and 9). The second two divisions have an additional parallel in that verses 5 and 9 are nearly identical in their wording. The first portion of the psalm (vv. 1–3) identifies the Lord as king, and then calls "the peoples" and the earth itself to "tremble" and "quake." The first declaration of God's kingship in Psalm 99 contains two statements that need some explanation: first, verse 1 says that Yahweh "sits" or is "enthroned" "above the cherubim." The word cherubim here refers to the creatures that adorned the top of the ark of the covenant, the ornate chest that originally carried the law given by God to Moses. These creatures were thought to support God's throne.

Second, the locale of the ark and of God's throne is Zion, that is, Jerusalem. One cannot understand God's kingship in the Psalms apart from this geographical identity. Jerusalem is Yahweh's "holy mountain" (v. 9); the

> The presence of God was thought to hover above the ark; see 1 Samuel 3:2–14.

center of the earth (Ezek. 5:5; 38:8–12; Psalm 48) from which God rules over all nations. Again, this concept is consistent with some other parts of the Old Testament, particularly the parts of Isaiah written during the exile. Isaiah 2:1–4 depicts Jerusalem to be the place into which all nations someday will stream to learn Yahweh's *torah*.

Having a sense of a place that is holy may be a foreign idea to many Christians. However, a holy place is an important part of biblical heritage that should be reclaimed. Associating a place with holiness stems from a people's experience of the Holy One in that place. Therefore, the location helps people

> "The LORD is thrice holy: in supreme majesty, in justice, and in responsibility."
> —James L. Mays, *Psalms*, Interpretation, 316.

recognize God as holy. This is the main idea in the conclusion to Psalm 99: "Worship at his holy mountain, for the LORD our God is holy." The people are called to praise his "great and awesome name," where "name" represents Yahweh's character, the essence of God.

God, the Righteous Judge

The second part of the psalm (vv. 4–5) describes the Lord as a "lover of justice." The Lord ensures justice and righteousness in Jacob (an alternative name for Israel; see Gen. 35:9–15). God's provision of justice is consistent with the ideal of royalty in the ancient Near East (Ps. 72:1–4). Psalm 97:2b declares, "righteousness and justice are the foundation of his throne," meaning that Yahweh is a judge without corruption or partiality. Moreover, Psalms 96:13 and 98:9 speak of God's judgment over the whole world. The New Testament borrows these descriptions of God as judge to create a portrait of a final judgment when Jesus will sit as sovereign arbiter of the fate of nations (Matt. 25:31–46).

The final portion of the psalm (vv. 6–9) praises God as one who answers the call of those who turn to him, a characteristic consistent with the portrait of ancient Near Eastern royalty. These verses recall Israel's helplessness, their cries to God, and the Lord's answer (v. 6). Yahweh does no less than what is expected of human kings as well; God listens to those in distress, and comes to their aid (Ps. 72:4, 12–14). Psalm 99:6–7 relates this provision of protection to the concrete experiences of Israel under the leadership of Moses, Aaron, and Samuel. God's watchful care, however, carries expectations. Israel is required to obey the decrees of the Lord. *Torah* provides a set of requirements that Israel must observe to maintain the favor of its sovereign. Thus, God's role as judge is not a biased perspective whereby Israel automatically benefits. Rather, having God as judge means meeting strict standards of obedience.

A God of All People

"[This psalm] seems a wondering, awed exclamation that the God of all peoples works justice and answers prayers for this particular people who are permitted to call him 'our God.' " —James L. Mays, *Psalms*, Interpretation, 315.

Like all the psalms that celebrate Yahweh's kingship, Psalm 99 has a universal scope. Yahweh is described as a ruler over all nations, not just Israel. Yahweh "is exalted over the peoples" (v. 2). These psalms are similar to the portion of Isaiah (Isaiah 40–55) that was written during the Babylonian exile (587–539 B.C.). The prophet declares that Yahweh is the sovereign over all nations and all historical events. Psalm 99 has the same assumption. Yet the psalm adds a more personal level to the awesome rule of God. The God who controls the whole cosmos is also the one who Israel confesses to be "*our* God" (vv. 5, 8, 9).

A Holy God

Throughout Psalm 99 one hears of the holiness of the divine king, which is most evident in the three refrains (vv. 3, 5, cf. v. 9): "Holy is he." Not only is the Lord holy, but also those things that come in contact with God, or are chosen for a special purpose, are holy. So the psalm calls Zion the "holy mountain" (v. 9). God's holiness, which is separate from creation, causes that created order to quake in the divine presence (v. 1). However, although evoking awe, God is present in specific and concrete ways. God chose a city (Zion) from which to rule; God calls worshipers to that locale; God listens to and answers the cries of a specific people (Israel). This rare expression of the divine presence might be called "incarnational"; that is, the God who is unlike humans, who has no human limitations, has nevertheless been made known in human history. The specific presence of God in Israel's communal life was incarnate in the fullest possible way in Jesus of Nazareth. He will bring the kingdom of God to fruition at the end of time, and perfect the seeds of divine rule planted during his ministry.

> **On Earth as It Is in Heaven**
>
> Artur Weiser comments that the repeated refrain of "Holy" was probably sung by an earthly choir as an "echo of the divine epiphany and revelation." —*The Psalms, Old Testament Library*, 641.

Context in the Psalter

Not only the message of Psalm 99 but its location in the Psalter are important. Psalm 99 appears in a group of psalms about Yahweh's kingship (Psalms 93; 95–99) that has Psalm 100 as a conclusion. No doubt these psalms were placed together because of their shared language about God's character as heavenly monarch. What is less apparent is the purpose of the placement of the enthronement psalms in the fourth major division of the Psalter (Psalms 90–106).

Book 4 appears in a strategic location immediately after a lament over the fall of the Davidic monarch (Ps. 89) that marks the end of Book 3 of the Psalter. Also, book 4 begins with the only song attributed to Moses (Psalm 90). Interestingly, the psalms that follow in Book 4 include seven references to the name of Moses (Psalm 90:1 [in the heading]; 99:6; 103:7; 105:26; 106:16, 23, 32), one of them in Psalm 99, with only one other occurrence in the rest of the book of Psalms. Perhaps those who put the Psalter together wished to answer the problem of the failure of the Davidic king by reminding the people of that foundational period when Israel had no king except Yahweh. During the exodus and wilderness wandering, Yahweh served as the sole ruler of the nation. God revealed the statutes and ordinances to Moses, and God guided the people to the promised land. The enthronement psalms begin (Ps. 93:3) and end (Ps. 99:7) with psalms that speak of God's decrees given to Moses. Psalm 99 and the neighboring enthronement psalms declare God as the only ruler worthy of complete trust. Only the divine king deserves confidence because only God is truly just and reliable.

Does King as Metaphor Communicate Today?

Can the image of God as king contribute to Christian life and faith? The question is important because some argue that this metaphor should not continue as a central Christian image. They cite as reasons several concerns: first, many people of faith have no experience with ruling monarchs, so the image of God as king is not a meaningful picture. Second, even if the image of a monarch is understood, in the eyes of many monarchy is inherently oppressive. To use kingship language for God ambushes the Christian picture of the divine. Part of that criticism comes from an understanding that the warrior image is inconsistent with Christian ideals. Third, some claim that belief in God as ruler of the world is naive. With the proliferation of tragedies in life, God seems far from "in control."

The kingship metaphor may be inaccessible to many people; nevertheless, the picture of God as a king is central to the Bible. Not everyone owns sheep, but few complain that to speak of God as shepherd is meaningless. The idea that a kingship is necessarily oppressive misses the nuance of a *divine* kingship. By definition, an ideal king in the ancient Near Eastern world would have been a liberator. No king ever lived up to that ideal, and that is precisely the point. The enthronement psalms declare that the divine King does what no human king ever does: rules in perfect justice, with special care and protection of the poor and helpless. Furthermore, to say that "the Lord is king" is not to say "the Lord is just like a human king," even an ideal human king. Divine kingship is not limited to, or defined by, human rule. The view of God as king transcends all human institutions, as evidenced by the fact that God's kingship includes the role of creator. Perhaps we should add that the divine institution of monarchy transcends gender as well. Even though the Psalms use the masculine designation "king," this derives from familiar social circumstances, not anything about the nature of God.

> "The psalm praises the LORD as a ruler who does answer." —James L. Mays, *Psalms*, Interpretation, 316.

Can talking about God's justice and God as a liberating ruler be undermined by the warrior image? Does not this metaphor encourage Christians to be warlike, even though Jesus commanded us to love our enemies? Not necessarily. There is no call for humans to take up arms in this or any of the enthronement psalms. The psalms present God as the warrior. If that point is taken seriously, perhaps the conclusion will be that vengeance, final judgment, and the structure of the universe must be left to God. Given the reality of human sinfulness, and the human inability to judge with equity, is it not good news that the one truly in charge is perfectly just? Also, as mentioned in the opening illustration, whether consciously or not, humans will always be "ruled" by something. The kingship psalms call for the affirmation of God as ruler consciously, rather than allowing the values of the culture, or delusions about human wisdom and power, to rule by default.

 Want to Know More?

About God as warrior and king? See James L. Mays, *Psalms*, Interpretation (Louisville, Ky.: John Knox Press, 1994), 225–29; for a more technical discussion, see Horst Dietrich Preuss, *Old Testament Theology*, vol. 1, Old Testament Library (Louisville, Ky.: Westminster John Knox Press, 1995), 128–30, 152–59.

About cherubim and the ark of the covenant? See Walther Eichrodt, *Theology of the Old Testament*, vol. 2, Old Testament Library (Philadelphia: Westminster Press, 1967), 202–5; Werner H. Schmidt, *The Faith of the Old Testament: A History* (Philadelphia: Westminster Press, 1983), 113–16.

About the "hiddenness" of the kingdom? See Robert H. Stein, *The Method and Message of Jesus' Teachings*, rev. ed. (Louisville, Ky.: Westminster John Knox Press, 1994), 76–81.

Those who do not make a conscious choice to be ruled by God will inevitably be governed by something that is oppressive, unscrupulous, or unrighteous.

Perhaps the best argument against the use of the kingship metaphor is the apparent lack of control by God in our world. The kingdom of God seems a bust, or at least wildly haywire. After witnessing the likes of wars, bombings, and the shootings of school children, perhaps the metaphor of a mental ward with the patients in charge seems more appropriate. If the kingdom of God exists, there are times when its presence is hard to discern.

The Bible acknowledges this dilemma. The kingdom may not be evident. Some aspects of the kingdom are almost invisible or behind the scenes. In the Gospels, the kingdom is compared to the *smallest* seed (Mark 4:31), to yeast *hidden* in dough (Matt. 13:33), and to a treasure *buried* in a field (Matt. 13:44). Not all of the kingdom of God has been revealed. Some parts of the kingdom are "now," and others are "not yet." As in a play, the kingdom we see may be just the first act. As with a relationship, the kingdom exists today, but what is today is merely a glimpse of what can be. The kingdom in part is in our reality, and the kingdom complete will be a future reality. The familiar refrain from Handel's "Hallelujah Chorus" and Revelation 11:15 remind us that there is a point in God's timing when the voices of heaven will shout, "the kingdom of the world is become the kingdom of our Lord and of his Christ" (American Standard Version).

> "Insofar as all the odd ways we do [God's] will at this moment are at best half-baked and halfhearted, the kingdom is still a long way off." —Frederick Buechner, *Wishful Thinking*, 50.

A Psalm of Hope

The final brush strokes on the kingdom of God will be finished in the future. The events and tragedies of today are not the last word. Keeping that bright future in view gives shape and hope that might be unavailable otherwise. In C. S. Lewis's *The Silver Chair*, the character Puddleglum is tempted by the Emerald Witch to denounce his belief in Aslan and the magical world of Narnia, and to dismiss his belief as a child's fantasy. Puddleglum declares,

> I'm on Aslan's side even if there isn't any Aslan to lead it. I'm going to live as like a Narnian as I can even if there isn't any Narnia. (New York: Collier, 1970, page 159)

In the face of pressing evidence to the contrary, evidence that tempts even the stalwart to dismiss their belief as fantasy, Christian faith declares that the kingdom of God will come. In the meantime, belief in the kingdom gives hope to defend against the false notion that the future will not offer any more than the meager drudgery of today's world.

The kingdom of God lies ahead of us, casting a shadow over every aspect of life. To forget about the reality that the kingdom offers leads to despair and hopelessness. Christians await the fullness of God's kingdom described by Paul:

> "In an age which idolizes appraisal but is uncomfortable with praise, the Psalms allow us to understand that praise does not spring from a delusion that things are better than they are, but rather from the human capacity for hope and joy."
> —Kathleen Norris, *The Psalms*, x.

> He must reign until he has put all his enemies under his feet. The last enemy to be destroyed is death. (1 Cor. 15:25–26)

When the church sings hymns like "Come, Thou Almighty King" or "Rejoice, the Lord Is King," we claim the promise of the kingdom. Though unseen in fullness, the kingdom of God is more real and more meaningful than any other power, even the power of death. So the church can join with the psalmist and shout, "The LORD rules!"

Questions for Reflection

1. What rules in your life? In this unit, the statement is made that we all are ruled by something, and if the ruler is not God, then it is "oppressive, unscrupulous, or unrighteous." What does that phrase mean? Evaluate the truthfulness of such a claim.
2. Like so many psalms, this psalm introduces ideas in tension, one of which is the image of God as warrior. How do you reconcile the notion of God as a holy warrior with Jesus' command to "turn the other cheek"?
3. Another tension in this psalm is the concept that God is ruler and loves justice, yet we see that chaos and injustice "reign" today. How do you reconcile the clash of believing in the ultimate lordship of God in a world that is out of control? What word of hope, if any, does Psalm 99 offer?
4. This psalm mentions the earth trembling and quaking in God's

holy presence. What are some other references in the Bible to trembling or quaking? (Use a Bible concordance if necessary.) What do these references communicate about the relationship of creation to God?

7

The Pilgrimage of Life

In the classic film *The Sound of Music*, the high point comes when the von Trapp family flees their native Austria. With German soldiers in pursuit, the family hides in the convent where Maria once resided when she was a nun. The troops enter the convent, forcing the von Trapps to escape through a rear exit. As they hurry out the back, they come quickly to what appears to be a dead end. Seemingly in a hopeless situation, Maria exclaims (in King James English), "I will lift up mine eyes to the hills from whence cometh my help!" (Ps. 121:1). Inspired by this confident affirmation, the von Trapps slip away and cross the border into the Swiss Alps—evidently the "hills" that Maria had in mind.

It is not surprising that, in her distress, Maria appealed to the first verse of Psalm 121. This verse is one of the best known in the Psalter, and when a verse is known by heart, it can easily be called

> "This psalm is an unqualified song of trust in the LORD's help." —James L. Mays, *Psalms*, Interpretation, 390.

upon in a moment of need. Surprisingly, though, knowing a Bible verse well can sometimes be a liability. When a verse is familiar, the meaning seems too obvious, and this familiarity tempts us to avoid the hard work of good interpretation. The measure of a good biblical understanding is fidelity to the text. Even though a psalm can have numerous legitimate applications because the language is poetic and flexible, not every interpretation is equally faithful to the central intent of the text. Some limits should be applied.

So, recognizing that good interpretation has limits, how should Psalm 121 be interpreted? Was Maria's understanding of this psalm, as she escaped "to the hills," a good one? In order to know, we must ask two basic questions: (1) What was the original setting for this psalm? and (2) What picture of God underlies this psalm?

The Setting

Psalm 121 is unusual because it gives a clue to the original setting in its title, "A Song of Ascents." In both English and Hebrew, the meaning of the word "ascents" is somewhat ambiguous, but a variation of the same term is found in the very next psalm, Psalm 122:4, in a reference to a ritual journey to Jerusalem (see also Ezra 7:9 and Ps. 24:3). This strongly suggests that Psalm 121 was used by pilgrims as a "traveling song," as they made their way up to Jerusalem, ascending to the holy city. Indeed, Psalm 121 is placed with similar psalms, grouped for that very purpose (Psalms 120–134, which, as a group, are called "songs of ascent"). In its original setting, then,

The road to Jerusalem

Psalm 121 was probably chanted by pilgrims moving along the road ascending to Jerusalem and was not used as a cry of distress like Maria's. (She might have quoted more appropriately from Psalms 3, 7, or 142, which are indeed "psalms of trouble," works set during the time of Saul's pursuit of David.)

The pilgrims in ancient Israel who uttered Psalm 121 would have been on their way up to Jerusalem for one of the holy feasts, most of which lasted for several days. In fact, when the celebration of a feast was combined with travel time to and from Jerusalem, the total festivities could last several weeks. Therefore, the Old Testament speaks of festival "seasons" (NRSV: "appointed feasts"). Today, in a symbolic way, the church preserves Psalm 121 as a song for pilgrims journeying to a feast by placing it in the lectionary in late October, in the time before Advent and Christmas. Positioned this way, Psalm 121 is a pilgrim song of the church, preparing Christians each year for the weeks of "pilgrimage," mentally and spiritually, to the celebration of Christ's coming.

Beyond the reference to "ascents" in the title, the body of Psalm 121 also offers clues about the psalm's original setting. One telltale sign is the way the pronouns shift from first person in verses 1–2 ("I" and "my") to second person in verses 3, 5–8 ("you" and "your"). This shift is a clue that Psalm 121 was used as a worshipful responsive chant, probably uttered either as the pilgrims started their journey to Jerusalem or at the close of the festival as the pilgrims left the Temple and made their way home. The first part of the chant (verses 1–2, and possibly verse 4) seems to be voiced by one of the pilgrims, who represents the whole company of travelers. The second part of the psalm would have been spoken in response by another voice. If the original setting of the psalm was the initial departure for Jerusalem, this second part could have been voiced by a travel leader, or perhaps one who is remaining at home. If the setting was the departure from the Temple, the latter part of the psalm was probably uttered by a priest at the Temple.

Understanding the original setting and use of this psalm in the pilgrim festivals can remind us today that God's people are still a band of pilgrims and that the journey of faith is a community affair. Moreover, knowing that the psalm was used in the holy seasons of Israel's worship can also be a valuable insight for the church. Faith is nurtured in the rhythms and festivals of the Christian year. The observance of seasons like Advent and Lent and of holy days like Christmas and Easter corresponds to the ancient festivals of Israel. The cycles of the church's calendar celebrate the fact that faith is strengthened by moments of keen awareness of the visitation of God. Traveling the pilgrim road of such seasons as Advent and Lent each year helps give pace and direction to the life of faith. It reminds us in the "ordinary days" that the God "who keeps Israel will neither slumber nor sleep" (Ps. 121:4).

Portrait of God

What picture of God do we see in Psalm 121? In order to discern the understanding of God that permeates this psalm, we need to correct a common misunderstanding of the first verse. In *The Sound of Music*, Maria uttered that verse as a statement of confidence: "I will lift up mine eyes to the hills from whence cometh my help!"

However, the Hebrew of the psalm treats that verse as a question: "I lift up my eyes to the hills—from where will my help come?" This rhetorical question sets up the affirmation of faith in verse 2: "My help comes from the LORD."

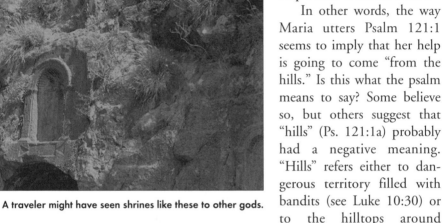

A traveler might have seen shrines like these to other gods.

In other words, the way Maria utters Psalm 121:1 seems to imply that her help is going to come "from the hills." Is this what the psalm means to say? Some believe so, but others suggest that "hills" (Ps. 121:1a) probably had a negative meaning. "Hills" refers either to dangerous territory filled with bandits (see Luke 10:30) or to the hilltops around Jerusalem where shrines of other gods were located. (In the ancient mind, gods were thought to be tied to specific geographical locations. A god of a mountain would have absolute power on that mountain, or a god of a valley would have unrestricted power in that valley.) In either case, the answer to the question, "From where will my help come?" is a resounding, "Not from the hills!" Despite the fact that in 1 Kings 20:23 Yahweh is described as a "god of the hills" (a designation that is refuted within the same story in 1 Kings 20; see also Jer. 3:23), that does not seem to be the intention here.

Indeed, as the pilgrim casts a wary eye toward the treacherous hills and wonders "from where will my help come?" the psalm provides the reassurance that "help comes from the LORD, who made heaven and earth" (Ps. 121:2). Though appearing only once in this psalm, this reference to God as creator of heaven and earth is very important. The same description occurs in two of the other psalms grouped in the songs of ascent (Pss. 124:8; 134:3), with the last occurrence possibly acting as a conclusion to the whole collection (Psalms 120–134). The phrase "maker of heaven and earth" is, therefore, a central tenet of faith in the songs of ascent.

> Many translations of Psalm 121:1 rely heavily on that of Martin Luther, who translated the phrase "from where my help comes" as a relative clause, instead of as a question, "From where will my help come?" which is a more accurate translation.

So, as the pilgrims traveled on their way to Jerusalem, even if their journey was only from another region of Israel, they surely observed worship sites (in "the hills") devoted to other deities—gods perhaps believed by their adherents to have ordered the cosmos. Thus, to confess that their God, Yahweh, was "maker of heaven and earth" was a declaration that these other deities were inferior to the Lord. The phrase "maker of heaven and earth" is one of the primary confessions of the church, found in the Apostles' Creed. Here, too, it stands not only as an affirmation of the true God but also as a renunciation of the false gods who dwell "in the hills" of our own culture. For example, the secularization of society leads to the popular falsehood that human technology and progress prove God nonexistent, or at least make God irrelevant. Today, in the presence of these secular "deities," the faithful are challenged to affirm that God is still sovereign, still "the maker of heaven and earth," just as ancient Israelites professed Yahweh to be the only power ultimately in control of the universe.

This comparison of Yahweh to other deities continues in verses 3–4, where it is declared that Israel's God "does not sleep or slumber." Here Yahweh is called, "keeper," the most prevalent description for God in the psalm (appearing six times). Israel's neighbors commonly believed that their gods "slept" (or died) during winter months and were revived in seasons of growth and harvest. Israel emphatically rejected this; Yahweh never slumbers, never stops keeping watch over Israel.

The idea that God keeps constant watch over Israel and its pilgrims is in-

> ### Can gods fall asleep?
>
> After their sacrifice remained untouched, Elijah taunted the worshipers of Baal at Mount Carmel and accused their god of sleeping (1 Kings 18:27).

tensified by the alternation of speakers in these two verses. One possible way to reconstruct the dialogue is that the first speaker, one of the pilgrims traveling to Jerusalem, says "My help comes from the LORD" (v. 2). Then a second voice, perhaps a worship leader, replies, in effect, "May he not let your foot slip; may your keeper not sleep" (v. 3). Then the pilgrim responds, "Indeed! He neither sleeps nor slumbers. (He is) the keeper of Israel" (v. 4). In essence, then, the psalm renders its claims about God by playing them off against two false ideas: Does Israel's help come from the "gods of the hills"? No, help comes only from Yahweh, maker of heaven and earth! Does Yahweh ever fall asleep like those other gods? No, the God who keeps Israel never slumbers!

So the "big picture" of God in this psalm is of one who created the cosmos, who helps Israel, and who, unlike the gods of other peoples, never fails to keep watch. But people of faith need to know that the "big picture" of God speaks to the small places of our everyday lives. By using the common poetic device of parallelism, Psalm 121 allows these large beliefs about God to become smaller, more personal comforts as well. The vast claim that God is "maker of heaven and earth" (121:2b) is set parallel to the conviction that God is "my help" (121:1b). The large-scale proclamation that God is concerned about the whole people, that God is the "keeper of Israel" (121:4b), is placed alongside the more personal truth that God is "your keeper" (121:3b). Thus, the pilgrim confesses the faith that the one who ordered the universe and who keeps Israel from harm is also a personal God who guides the steps of each person on pilgrimage to Jerusalem.

In the final four verses of the psalm, we are introduced to a new image of God: God as "shade." These verses are spoken again by a "worship leader," and they not only confess the faith of the speaker, but are said as a blessing on behalf of the pilgrims for their safekeeping as they travel. Verse 5 describes God as "your shade." This is, of course, a soothing figure of speech. Imagine how comforting it would be to a traveler in the heat of the Palestinian countryside to think of God as "shade." However, the picture of God as "shade" is more than just a consoling image; it is also a majestic one. In Psalm 36:7, Yahweh's "shade" or "shadow" is equated with the shelter or safety of the Temple, the seat of God's reign over the whole cosmos. So to describe God as "shade" is part of a larger portrayal of Yahweh as king, as one who has the power to rule, to shelter, and to protect (see Judg. 9:7–15).

In verse 6, we see hints of some of the difficult traveling conditions the pilgrim might face, and from which Yahweh protects: the sun by day, the moon by night. With the proximity of the mention of shade in the previous verse, the reference to the sun seems obvious. However, the mention of the moon may seem odd. The modern reader should remember that ancient people believed the moon could affect people adversely; they could become literally "moonstruck." However, more is involved than natural perils. Some ancient peoples con-

---

Ever been moonstruck?

Though the word often describes a dreamy or sentimental state, "moonstruck" also can describe someone who is mentally unbalanced. In fact, the English word "lunatic" comes from the Latin word for "moon."

sidered the sun and the moon deities: for example, the Egyptian Ra (the sun god) and the Mesopotamian Nanna (the moon god). So here, once again, as was the case in verses 1–4, the psalm probably reveals and highlights the pilgrims' struggle with other gods.

On the hilltops and in the sky, both day and night, Yahweh's followers are challenged by the power of rival deities. The psalm writer, however, makes plain that travelers are safe because of the watchful care of Yahweh. Verse 7 offers a final summary of protection "from all evil" with a line that is either a wish ("may he keep you") or a description of what will be ("he will keep you"). Verse 8 ends the psalm with a final reference to Yahweh's "keeping" vigil over future pilgrimages to the holy city ("coming in" and "going out").

"The Jew even today fixes a *mezuzah* on the portal of his house door, which he touches each time he goes in or comes out of his home. This is a small metal cylinder containing a piece of parchment on which are written the words of Deut. 6:4–9 and 11:13–21. As he touches it, he repeats the words of verse 8 of this Psalm." —George A. F. Knight, *Psalms*, vol. 2, Daily Study Bible (Philadelphia: Westminster Press, 1983), 266.

Traveling Mercies

Today we see Psalm 121 as intended to aid all pilgrims, not only those ancient travelers to Jerusalem but also contemporary people of faith who journey toward Christ in the church. Such a journey is made with full recognition of false gods all around who compete for devotion. Psalm 121 assures those travelers that the keeper of Israel is indeed the "maker of heaven and earth" and not a pretender. The recognition of God's power as creator also colors the celebration of the advent of "Jesus Christ, his only son, our Lord."

With these points in mind, consider again Maria of *The Sound of Music* and the question posed at the beginning of this unit about how to interpret this psalm. Was Maria's interpretation true to the text of Psalm 121:1? Was it historically accurate? In some ways, we must answer no, even though the words of Psalm 121:1 gave her dramatic and needed support in a time of crisis. Even so, we should add that Psalm 121, like most works in the Psalter, can take on a life all its own in the liturgy of the church and in the devotion of the faithful. For example, Psalm 121:1 is understood by many in light of 2 Kings 6:17, which tells of Elisha and his company, surrounded by the king of Aram and his army, having eyes opened to the vision of horses and fiery chariots on the mountain, that is, to divine help "in the hills." This connection, like Maria's, may be inaccurate historically, but what are we to say when a passage of scripture, like Psalm 121:1, though misapplied, still offers words of comfort to those who are distressed? Who can say how often believers have grappled for a word from God, and misinterpreted or misapplied what they found?

Want to Know More?

About feasts? See Donald K. McKim, *Westminster Dictionary of Theological Terms* (Louisville, Ky.: Westminster John Knox Press, 1996), 103; Barbara Smith, *The Westminster Concise Bible Dictionary* (Philadelphia: Westminster Press, 1981), 60–61; Werner H. Schmidt, *The Faith of the Old Testament: A History* (Philadelphia: Westminster Press, 1983), 117–27.

About idols and worship? See McKim, *Westminster Dictionary of Theological Terms*, 137; Alan Richardson and John Bowden, eds., *The Westminster Dictionary of Christian Theology* (Philadelphia: Westminster Press, 1983), 280–81.

About pilgrimages? See McKim, *Westminster Dictionary of Theological Terms*, 210; J. G. Davies, ed., *The Westminster Dictionary of Liturgy and Worship* (Philadelphia: Westminster Press, 1986), 433–37.

The writer Frederick Buechner tells of a low time in his life when despair had nearly overtaken him. In the midst of depression, he saw a car speed past with a customized license plate that read "TRUST." Buechner took this as a sign from God that he should place his life totally in God's hands. He did: his depression left him, and he went on with his life. Some time later, however, he discovered the car that delivered the profound message of "trust" actually belonged to one of his neighbors, an investment banker. The license plate message had no religious context. Yet who can say definitely that this license plate wasn't God's word for Buechner that day? (Frederick Buechner, *Telling Secrets: A Memoir* [San Francisco: HarperCollins, 1991], 49–50.)

It is ironic that both that five-letter word "trust" and Maria's cry, "I will lift up mine eyes to the hills from whence cometh my help!" were words taken *out* of context, but still were so powerful. Scripture is best interpreted *in* context. However, some verses seem to have power independent of their context, or of our ability to discern the context. By the grace of God, some texts provide strength for the living of these days even when applied imperfectly. For Maria, the majesty of the Alps probably reminded her of God's majesty. And maybe, in the final analysis, she was not too far from the original meaning of Psalm 121. In her mind, surely the God who created heaven and earth, who created those magnificent peaks, could deliver her family in their time of trouble. As with the pilgrims of old, she believed that the one who ordered the universe could keep her from harm, could provide "shade" in the heat of her distress. She was convinced that God was more powerful than the threat facing her, and for travelers ancient and modern, Psalm 121 affirms that the God who made heaven and earth is indeed stronger than any earthly peril.

 ## Questions for Reflection

1. This psalmist is aware that human beings are prone to place trust in false gods, and the psalm challenges us to trust in the Lord in the face of many other competing interests. What are those things in which contemporary people are tempted to trust?
2. The last two verses of Psalm 121 offer a promise of protection from evil. How realistic is this promise of God's protection in life's "going out and coming in"?
3. In this unit, mention is made of times when calling to mind scripture has been an encouragement to people of faith. What are some other scriptures that give encouragement?
4. This psalm probably was used as part of a pilgrim festival, a regular yearly trip to Jerusalem to worship in the Temple. What are some of the regular things done in worship throughout the year? Why are these things observed or practiced?

8 Psalm 8

What Does It Mean to Be Human?

The question, "What does it mean to be human?" introduces a huge subject that no one psalm can answer fully. Yet Psalm 8 addresses the question directly and perhaps more broadly than any work in the Psalter, maybe even any passage in the Bible. This psalm helps give a basic definition of who a human is in relation to God and the rest of God's creation. As such, Psalm 8 has tremendous potential to speak to issues that modern people describe as "ecological," that is, issues concerning care for the earth and its resources. Given the serious environmental questions and public policy debates related to these issues, this psalm provides a perspective to help Christians engage this set of problems. The stanzas of Psalm 8 reveal an understanding of the role humanity plays to care for the planet the way God intended.

"Where human beings once exploited nature thoughtlessly or in the belief that no great harm could be done to the environment, the twentieth century is leaving us with a transforming of such unconsciousness. We now recognize we have an intimate connection with air, water, soil, fire, everything." —Maria Harris, *Proclaim Jubilee: A Spirituality for the Twenty-first Century* (Louisville, Ky.: Westminster John Knox Press, 1996), 8.

Praise Ye the Lord

This psalm is a hymn. Recall from unit 2, "Types of Psalms," that hymn psalms have the sole purpose of praising the Lord. The psalm begins and ends with a telltale line that indicates this function: "O LORD, our Sovereign, how majestic is your name in all the earth!" However, Psalm 8 is different from other hymns in the Psalter because it speaks entirely to God. Unlike a typical hymn, this psalm does not include an invitation to praise God, but delves immediately into the act of praise and remains there throughout.

The hymn proper (counting the opening and closing lines as separate from the rest) has two unequal parts: verses 1b–2; 3–8. The first section is difficult to interpret; in fact, scholars are unsure of the meaning of these verses. Mays offers the following translation (65–66):

> Your splendor above the heavens is praised
>   from the mouth of babes and infants.
> You have established power because of your foes,
>   to quell enemy and avenger.

Although some uncertainty exists about the meaning of these lines, the phrase "above the heavens" suggests a clue. Recall the opening line of the psalm: "O LORD, our Sovereign, how majestic is your name *in all the earth.*" Verse 1b expands and elaborates on the opening line in at least two ways. First, it gives a complete picture of God's sovereignty and the realm in which God should be praised, namely in the earth (v. 1a), as well as in the heavens (v. 1b). Verse 1b implies that the Lord is not limited to the realm of humans but is the ruler over the universe from a throne above the earth. Second, it gives insight into the psalmist's picture of the universe, a "prescientific" worldview that understands heaven and earth to be separated by a dome, or "firmament" (see Gen. 1:6–8). The purpose of the dome is to hold back the waters above the earth (that periodically fall to earth in the form of rain) so that life on earth is possible. The psalmist believes God's throne rests on the waters above that dome (see Ps. 29:10). From this perch high above creation, God, in the psalmist's mind, sits enthroned as king over the universe. Therefore, the psalmist logically speaks of praising God not only on earth but in the heavenly realm (i.e., in God's royal court) as well.

> "The LORD is the cosmic sovereign whose majesty is visible in the whole world." — James L. Mays, *Psalms*, Interpretation, 65.

The phrase "from the mouth of babes and infants" (v. 2a) is also difficult to understand. Mays is probably right in saying that this is hyperbole, a poetically exaggerated way of saying that every human utterance is a response to the reign of God (66). In the final statement in this section (v. 2b), "enemy and avenger" probably refer to the forces of chaos that would threaten the order of God's creation. So this first section of the psalm borrows from the common ancient Near Eastern beliefs that creation was generated out of the defeat of chaos. This picture of the universe differs from that of much of the literature from Mesopotamia, Egypt, or Canaan, however, in that there is no hint of a battle between the Lord and other gods. Rather, the Lord exhibits complete mastery over all creation. As the psalm says in the next section, every portion of the universe is the "work of God's fingers" (v. 3a).

What Are Humans That You Are Mindful?

The second major portion of Psalm 8 (vv. 3–8) speaks in first-person voice. These verses are filled with wonder at the created order on the one hand, and the role of humanity within that order on the

The Earth is but a speck on the blanket of the universe.

other hand. Verse 3 considers again the heavens as the sphere of God's cosmic rule, turning sharply to question the place of humanity before the Lord. Two Hebrew words are used to refer to humans, both of which connote human frailty. The first word, *enosh*, comes from a root that means "to be in poor health"; the second expression, *ben-adam;* means literally "son of man." The word *adam*, from which the Bible gets the name of the first man in Genesis 2, is related to the word *adamah*, meaning "ground." A human is a finite creature, one made of dust, who returns to dust eventually (Gen. 3:19). Together these parallel terms serve to point out the weakness of humans in relation to God and the marvels of God's creation. The question of verse 4 could be paraphrased, "What is so special about these puny creatures that you would pay attention to them?" The intended answer to this rhetorical question would seem to be "Nothing." Compared to God, humans have nothing to boast about; they are limited in knowledge and ability, and in the end they are swallowed up in the ground from which they came.

A Little Lower than God

Despite this, however, God gave humans a unique place in the created order. The imagery of God's cosmic rule in this psalm is important because, as Mays says, humans have been given an "office" in God's kingdom (65). Verse 5 says that humans are made "a little lower than God" or "a little lower than the divine beings (i.e., angels)." The dispute over the translation of this line results from the fact that the common Hebrew word for God *(Elohim)* is a plural, and the same word can sometimes refer to the gods of the nations or members of Yahweh's royal court. Whatever the intention of the psalmist here, the claim for humanity is a grand one. Verses 6–8 define the expanse of human dominion. Human beings are in charge of "the works of God's hands," that is, the animals, both domestic and wild, and the birds of the air and the creatures in the seas.

This second section of the psalm is reminiscent of two other passages of scripture: first, the place reserved for humans here sounds much like Psalm 115:16, which states:

> The heavens are the LORD's heavens,
> but the earth he has given to human beings.

This amazing distribution of power points again to the royal office of humanity. This second part of Psalm 8, and to a lesser degree the whole psalm, also seems to have Genesis 1:26–28; 2:19–20 in mind. Genesis 1:26–28 twice states humanity's dominion over the animal kingdom. The classification of animals by their dwelling place—land, air, and water—is the same in Psalm 8 and Genesis 1:26–28. This point is important, for it provides a major key to how the psalmist thinks of humans being created in the "image of God." The divine image here is defined as the charge given humans over creation. God mastered chaos and "brought forth creation"; humanity is now given power over that creation "to bring forth civilization" (Mays, 67). This is striking, since in the ancient world, particularly in Egyptian texts, the king is said to bear the image of the gods, to serve as the gods' representative on earth. Psalm 8 seems to transfer that role to all humans.

> "God didn't just make us; God made us both a representation and representatives of the reign of the LORD to the other creatures." —James L. Mays, *Psalms,* Interpretation, 69.

71

One should not ignore the fact that the Davidic king maintains a special place in the Psalms (see Psalms 2; 45; 72; 110; 132). Although humanity as a whole is acknowledged here as having great responsibility, Yahweh's anointed never disappears from the Psalter. Mays perhaps says it best:

> The Davidic king is given dominion over the nations; humankind, over living creatures. The problem for one is the chaos of history; for the other, the chaos of wildness. The two are side by side in the Psalter. (67)

More discussion about the relationship between humanity as a whole and the "anointed of the Lord" (the king) as bearers of God's image will follow later in this unit.

Dominion over the Earth

On the surface, Psalm 8 seems to assign almost unlimited power to humanity to rule over God's creation. Certainly the text has been misread that way at times. In fact, some blame passages like Psalm 8 for the current environmental crises. They claim that the biblical text that speaks of "dominion" has been used as justification for modern industrialists and governments to "dominate" nature. But as the framing of the previous sentence implies, the problem has been more with the *interpretation* of the text's reference to dominion than with the text itself. Others have offered a more nuanced position that supposes texts like Psalm 8 (and Gen. 1:26–28) present a hierarchical relationship between humans and the rest of creation, a position that is counter to that of other Old Testament texts (like Gen. 2:4b–25) that explicitly present humans as creatures from the dust of the earth. Though perhaps more accurate than the former, this latter position still overlooks key features of Psalm 8 that could prevent flawed readings of this passage.

"The holy earth. We must take such care of it. It must take such care of us. This side of Paradise, we are each of us so nearly all the other has." —Frederick Buechner, *Whistling in the Dark: An ABC Theologized* (San Francisco: Harper & Row, 1988), 40.

The Earth Is the Lord's

The structure of the psalm is the first feature that should prevent humans from reading these verses as a license to do whatever they want with the earth. Remember that Psalm 8 begins and ends with praise of God: "O LORD, our Sovereign, how majestic is your name in all the earth" (vv. 1a, 9). Human dominion is framed, determined, and limited by the ultimate rule of God over all creation. This concept alone should give pause when we consider the blatant abuse of the earth in which every human has participated to some degree. During the early conflict over possession of land between Native Americans and the newly formed American government, some Native Americans issued eloquent statements against possession of large territories by the U.S. government. Though no written documentation exists of those speeches, the power of their words in secondhand reports speaks afresh today. They could

> "How can you buy or sell the sky, the warmth of the land?" —Ted Perry, professor and filmwriter, adapting words attributed to Chief Seattle in a speech from January 1854.

not understand how any people or government could argue that it "owned" land. Land could not be "had." Ground and dirt could not be possessed, any more than the sky, the sun, or water could be the "property" of an individual or group. The position of the Old Testament, and Psalm 8, differs slightly from Native American thought by drawing a sharp separation between the Creator and the creation. Nevertheless, this text has one important point in common with the Native American position: humans serve not as owners over creation, but as tenants. This is not to say that rights to private property ought to be overturned, but "ownership" in the ultimate sense is not determined by a deed.

A Just Rule

A second feature of Psalm 8 that should prevent this kind of abuse of creation is the royal image bestowed upon humanity. At first blush, this might seem ironic. Are not monarchs infamous for their absolute hegemony, tyrannical rule, and abuse of their subjects? Perhaps the answer would be yes if it were based on monarchical forms of government experienced throughout history. However, the ancient Near East had a royal ideal that was far different. A reading of Psalm 72 makes clear that ancient Israel shared its neighbors' conviction that a king's rule should ensure justice, equality, and protection for the whole kingdom (see unit 6 on Psalm 99, for further discussion). This royal ideal is in view in Psalm 8 as well. Thus, Mays states, "In the vision of the psalm, civilization is meant to be a vast project of stewardship" (69).

Other Citations

A final point that should ensure proper understanding of humanity's role over the created order is the appearance of the words of Psalm

8:4 in other biblical texts. Whether Psalm 8:4 is the original citation being quoted by the others or vice versa is not known. All may be citations of another well-known line. Regardless, the appearance of the words, "what are human beings that you are mindful of them, mortals that you care for them?" in other texts gives a slightly different understanding of these words. When these words appear in Psalm 144:3, they are followed by a rather negative portrait of humanity:

> They are like a breath;
> their days are like a passing shadow.

Instead of introducing humanity as God's coregents, Psalm 144 utilizes the question, "What are human beings?" to point out the vapid nature of human existence. Humans must depend solely on God, the psalm declares, since human power is ineffective. This seems in stark contrast to the more positive view of humanity in Psalm 8.

A second text that contains the words of Psalm 8:4 is Job 7:17. Job's context features a request to receive less attention from God.

Job indeed acknowledges the special place of humans in the divine order, but for Job this is a curse, not a blessing. So Job desires to be like one of the lesser creatures that merit less attention from the Almighty. Job's view is colored by his suffering. However, Job's view also indicates that having God "pay attention" to and "visit" us does not mean that God turns us loose with power to do whatever we wish in the world.

Job's use of the words suggests that divine visitation, the royal office of humans, involves more of responsibility than privilege. In sum, the question, "What are human beings?" should be read in the light of the overarching praise of God in Psalm 8. The glory and honor bestowed upon humans (Ps. 8:5) are received with surprise and the realization of humanity's unworthiness. Hubris (human pride), like that expressed at the Tower of Babel, misleads many to believe that they are independent caregivers of creation. What has been given to human charge, though, is much less—only a sublease. This realization provides a foundation for confronting current ecological problems. Texts like Psalm 8, when rightly interpreted, give Christians not only a charge but a manifesto to tackle this issue.

 Want to Know More?

About firmament and the Hebrew understanding of the universe? See Celia Brewer Marshall, *A Guide through the Old Testament* (Louisville, Ky.: Westminster John Knox Press, 1989), 24; Paul J. Achtemeier, ed., *Harper's Bible Dictionary* (San Francisco: Harper & Row, 1985), 309–10.

About the court of Yahweh? See Horst Dietrich Preuss, *Old Testament Theology*, vol. 1, Old Testament Library (Louisville, Ky.: Westminster John Knox Press, 1995), 256–58; see also Paul D. Hanson, *Isaiah 40–66*, Interpretation (Louisville, Ky.: John Knox Press, 1995), 15–23, and James L. Mays, *Psalms*, Interpretation (Louisville, Ky.: John Knox Press, 1994), 268–71.

About spirituality and ecology? See Sara Covin Juengst, *Like a Garden: A Biblical Spirituality of Growth* (Louisville, Ky.: Westminster John Knox Press, 1996), 33–46.

We Do See Jesus

Hebrews 2:5–9 is another text that includes the familiar words of Psalm 8:4. Without question, the writer of Hebrews quotes this psalm. In acknowledging humanity's unique place in the created order, Hebrews (like Psalm 144 and Job 7:17) again corrects the supposition that humans are free agents, left to do and be whatever they want. Rather, Hebrews holds up a portrait of what humanity is intended to be. Simply put, the intention of God for every person is Christ. We should be like him. Hebrews 2:8 states, "we do not yet see everything in subjection to them [humans]," but (v. 9) "we do

75

see Jesus." Jesus alone gives the example where dominion did not, and will not, become domination. He alone gives an accurate picture of God's ultimate rule. When all things are finally put under his feet, then all will see creation cared for in the way God intends.

What does it mean to be human? Despite conflicting messages from media and culture, the words of Psalm 8 tie the meaning of humanity to the care of creation.

? Questions for Reflection

1. What makes humans distinct from the rest of creation?
2. In commenting on Psalm 8:2, this unit quotes Mays to say that "every human utterance is a response to . . . God." What does that mean? How true is that comment?
3. This psalm is a hymn directly addressing God. What are some of the attributes and accomplishments associated with God? What are some of the attributes and accomplishments associated with humans?
4. Speaking out against something or stepping in to take part in a cause can be difficult. A common response is, "That's none of my business." What challenge does this psalm offer?

Praying Anger

"**Y**ou'll pay for this, I swear. As God is my witness, you'll pay." The craving for justice, particularly retributive justice, is very strong in humans, and God is seen as the one who should dispense that justice. This desire can be seen in our own responses to a story about a former guard of a Nazi death camp who fled to Bolivia to avoid arrest. He loathed having a fugitive's lack of freedom, but comforted himself by regularly visiting an art museum. He found solace in a painting of a lone fisherman on a placid lake. He longed to be the fisherman in that picture because his past haunted him. Even there in the museum was a painting of a crucified Jew on the opposite wall, a memorial to those who died in the Holocaust. The former guard's fear of being discovered increased when a Holocaust survivor, who had come to view the crucifixion scene, engaged him in conversation and probed him about his past.

On one occasion, as he gazed on the painting of the fisherman, he actually became part of the picture! For as long as his imagination allowed, the man fished without care of being apprehended. He repeated this with every visit to the museum. He prayed to God to become a permanent part of the scene. "Wait," we might cry.

What do we do with our anger?

"If there is any justice, God can not grant that prayer!"

One night police pursued him. He had been identified, and, if arrested, he would pay at last for the suffering he had inflicted on so many Jews. He fled to the museum, hoping that God might grant his prayer and help him escape. The museum was closing and the lights were out. He burst in and headed for the wall where the painting hung. Rushing down the dark corridors toward the serene picture, he prayed that God would make him a permanent part of the scene on the wall. He came to the location, and in the darkness knelt and again made his request. When the museum guards arrived a few seconds later and turned on the lights, the man was not there. God had answered the prayer! But what the fugitive had not seen in the darkness was that his painting had been moved. In its place hung the painting of the crucified Jew. The placid lake had been replaced with a cruel cross, and the former killer was doomed to suffer as he had made others suffer.

A Desire for Vengeance

Psalm 137 contains the wish for retribution, and it belongs to a group of poems sometimes called "imprecatory psalms." Though not a formal category identified by style or structure, this label is given because these psalms wish for an enemy's disaster. The desire for vengeance is startling both because of a seeming contradiction with Jesus' command to "love your enemies," and because the cry for vengeance is part of a prayer, a direct address to God. Yet wishing for an adversary's annihilation is not uncommon in the Psalter, and in fact it seems to be an integral part of psalmic prayer. With no apparent qualms, Psalm 58:10–11 predicts the rejoicing of the righteous over the death of the wicked:

> "The psalm is of course an embarrassment to us, because of its 'lethal' ending. And yet every pastor knows about folk with exactly such rage, and for exactly the same reasons. We seethe, as did they, over unfair losses that leave us displaced and orphaned." —Walter Brueggemann, *Cadences of Home: Preaching among Exiles* (Louisville, Ky.: Westminster John Knox Press, 1997), 5.

The righteous will rejoice when they see vengeance done;
  they will bathe their feet in the blood of the wicked.
People will say, "Surely there is a reward for the righteous;
  surely there is a God who judges on earth."

Psalm 137 is the clearest example of this type of psalm. It contains one of the angriest wishes for retribution of any psalm, and that

prompts several questions: Can a psalm like this fit into the practice
and theology of Christian prayer? Isn't this psalm completely at odds
with biblical visions of world peace and the teachings of Jesus? How
does one deal with the inclusion of Psalm 137 in scripture?

The Setting

The psalm divides neatly into three parts. Verses 1–4 reveal the historical setting of the song with a clear reference to an event in Israel's
corporate life, the Babylonian exile. In 587 B.C. King Nebuchadnezzar of Babylon destroyed Jerusalem and took the leading citizens
into captivity. The psalm reflects this in the opening line:

> By the rivers of Babylon—
>> there we sat down and there we wept
>> when we remembered Zion.   (v. 1)

The past-tense verb "sat" and the directive "there" seem to indicate
Psalm 137 was actually composed after the exile when the people of
Judah returned to their land (after 539 B.C. when King Cyrus of Per-
sia conquered the Babylonians). However, the experience of exile
lingers in the mind of the writer; the wound is still fresh. In this first
section the voice is plural ("we sat down"). Those uttering the psalm
are probably the select group of Israelites (Levites) who once made
music in the Temple. Their lamentation takes the symbolic form of
"hanging up their harps" (the harp or lyre was a stringed instrument
held in one hand and plucked or strummed with the other; see 1
Samuel 16:14–23). This identification of speakers intensifies the
grief over the loss of Jerusalem, since the Levites had more formal
ties to the holy city and the Temple than ordinary citizens. These
musicians were the particular targets of their captors, who taunted
them saying, "Sing us one of the songs of Zion" (v. 3). The songs
mentioned here may refer to any song praising Yahweh. However,
there is a group of psalms that scholars label "Zion songs" (Psalms
46; 48; 76; 84; 87; 122) that the writer could have in mind. These
psalms all praise the beauty of Zion and the Temple; they celebrate
God's choice of Zion/Jerusalem as the divine dwelling place. Zion
and the Temple are objects of the psalmists' longing, an idea expressed well by Psalm 84:10:

> For a day in your courts is better
>   than a thousand elsewhere.
> I would rather be a doorkeeper in the house of my God
>   than live in the tents of wickedness.

Some of the Zion songs also declared that Zion was invincible (Psalm 48), a tenet seriously shaken by the events of 587 B.C. The memory of these songs would have added to the pain of Jerusalem's distance and state of disrepair. The Levites would have recalled these events after their return to a city and Temple that remained a heap of rubble. In Babylon, they remembered Zion as the city of God, standing strong and glorious on the hill of Yahweh's choosing. Now they could *only* continue to remember this city because of the ruins that remained (84:6).

Singing a Song of Faith

Verse 4 of Psalm 137 is connected to the previous verse by the repetition of the words "sing" and "song(s)." The speakers ask, "How could we sing the LORD's song in a foreign land?" The issue is not the literal inability to sing but the content and purpose of their singing. The "songs of Zion," whatever their identity, would have contained claims about Yahweh as ruler of the cosmos (from Zion). These claims would be impossible to make, indeed would seem ridiculous, with Zion razed and God's people in a land controlled by foreign deities. So the request for these singers to produce a song of Zion was a taunt with the inherent claim that Israel's God was powerless. As Mays states, "the issue was not music; it was faith" (422).

"The singers are very clear that the issue is not where they are but whether the LORD rules in the world in which they live." — James L. Mays, *Psalms*, Interpretation, 423.

The exile of 587 B.C. posed particular challenges for Israel's faith. Jerusalem's destruction signaled for many the invalidity of belief in Yahweh. If Yahweh were powerful, surely God's people would not have been defeated! Exile must mean that Yahweh is subordinate to the Babylonian gods. This is one ancient form of the timeless problem of evil and suffering, a problem that must be dealt with constructively in any religious faith. Israel responded by declaring that the exile was Yahweh's punishment of God's own people, and that the nations merely served as Yahweh's instruments of chastisement (Isa. 10:5–19). This answer might not satisfy modern Christians, but clearly good things do not always happen to good people. One of the weaknesses of some popular Christianity is the emphasis on an individual's success as a measure of faith. "If my faith is strong," some believe, "I will be healed" or "my business will prosper." Israel's experience should be enough to dispel these notions.

The Memory of Jerusalem

The words "forget" and "remember" are the key terms in verses 5–6, the second major division of the psalm. Here one of the Levites speaks on behalf of the group. The lines, "If I forget you, O Jerusalem" and "if I do not remember" express the calling to reclaim what has been lost in Jerusalem's destruction. "Remembering" is perhaps defined by the final expression in verse 6, "if I do not set Jerusalem above my highest joy." The memory here is not of a Jerusalem far away but of a Jerusalem that once was. In fact, the proximity of the speaker to the holy city, given its devastated condition, makes the situation even more painful. The speaker has the memory of a way of life whose center was found in worship in the Jerusalem Temple. The Levitical voice in the psalm asks for a Temple singer's ultimate punishment if he fails to recall Jerusalem in all its glory: the hand that plays the lyre will wither; the tongue that sings Yahweh's praise will cling to the roof of his mouth. This memory is a primary key to survival. Throughout history, prisoners of war, political exiles, and refugees have endured their plight because they had strong memories (of a place, of family, of scripture) that sustained them.

Righteous Anger

The emphasis on Jerusalem is the primary key to understanding the anger with which the psalm concludes and the passion of the prayer of vengeance. The psalmist's memory of Zion is not simple nostalgia or homesickness. Rather, the loss of Jerusalem and the Temple marked a theological tragedy. A perusal of the Zion songs (Psalm 46; 48; 76; 84; 87; 122) gives some idea of the writer's beliefs about this place. Zion is the "city of the great King" and the "joy of all the earth" (Ps. 48:2); the center of world peace (Ps. 76:3) and justice (Ps. 122:5). Zion is the "cosmic mountain," having a significance for the world that no other location can claim. This is the place that has been destroyed by the Babylonians.

The centrality of Zion for the psalmist has few, if any, modern Western parallels. However, in Charles Frazier's *Cold Mountain*, there is a hint of this kind of fixation on a place that anchors all of life. The central character of the novel, Inman, is making his way home to Cold Mountain near the end of the Civil War. That particular location in the Blue Ridge mountains of North Carolina was for Inman the center of life. As he makes his way back there, Inman recalls a Cherokee called Swimmer he met when they were both sixteen:

Want to Know More?

About the exile to Babylon? See Celia Brewer Marshall, *A Guide through the Old Testament* (Louisville, Ky.: Westminster John Knox Press, 1989), 108–21.

About the problem of evil and suffering? See Shirley C. Guthrie, *Christian Doctrine*, rev. ed. (Louisville, Ky.: Westminster John Knox Press, 1994), 166–91; Tyron L. Inbody, *The Transforming God: An Interpretation of Suffering and Evil* (Louisville, Ky.: Westminster John Knox Press, 1997).

About the imprecatory psalms? See Erich Zenger, *A God of Vengeance? Understanding the Psalms of Divine Wrath* (Louisville, Ky.: Westminster John Knox Press, 1996).

> Swimmer had looked out at the landforms and said he believed Cold Mountain to be the chief mountain of the world. Inman asked how he knew that to be true, and Swimmer had swept his hand across the horizon to where Cold Mountain stood and said, Do you see a bigger'n? (New York: Atlantic Monthly Press, 1997, 14).

The immensity of Cold Mountain was more in the heart than in any topographical data, and so also was Zion.

The loss of the place Ezekiel called the "navel of the earth" (Ezek. 38:12) produced a righteous anger that can only be appreciated in the context of a similar theological and spiritual devastation. Are there acts of evil of such magnitude as to produce anger that should not ebb quickly? Indeed. There are times when to forgive too quickly would be to forget the precious thing that has been lost. This is the dilemma the psalmist faces in Psalm 137. To immediately express love for the Babylonians would mean to wipe Jerusalem from his mind. Although, that is not to say that forgiveness could not come eventually.

A professor taught at an institution that underwent a quick and nearly complete administrative change. In the wake of that upheaval, the professor and many fellow faculty members were forced to find new places of service. Several years passed. Though each located another position in a good school, the pain of the forced exodus still remained. Whenever they gathered, the only topic of conversation for this group of colleagues seemed to be the injustice of those events. Many other professors who had not suffered through the same turmoil thought this fixation on the past was unhealthy and counterproductive to the work of the present. What the unexiled failed to see was that the professors' anger persisted because something that need not have been lost *was* lost. The center of their world collapsed, and forgiveness was simply not an immediate option. The professors remembered their former place as the psalmists remembered Zion.

The Call for Justice

The final portion of Psalm 137 (vv. 7–9) is a prayer. Here the psalmist addresses the Lord with a word that recurs throughout the psalm: "Remember!" The particular request is for God to recall the Edomites who became Babylon's partners in Jerusalem's fall. Verses 8–9 then turn to the immediate agent in Zion's destruction: Babylon. The psalmist looks forward to that day when the Lord metes out justice to all nations. Surely then Babylon and Edom will get their due. In wishing and hoping for this, Psalm 137 enters the context of prophetic oracles against these nations (Isa. 34:1–17;

The Eternal Flame at the Holocaust Museum in Washington D.C.

47:1–15; Jer. 49:7–22; 51:1–58; Ezek. 35:1–15; Obadiah).

Psalm 137 concludes with what is perhaps the most shocking statement in scripture:

> Happy shall they be who take your little ones
> and dash them against the rock!

As Mays notes, military campaigns sometimes included the slaughter of children when the goal was the removal of a whole population (423; see 2 Kings 8:12; Hos. 10:14; Nahum 3:10). This line is the second of two beatitudes that have the Hebrew word *ashre* at their beginning. As noted in unit 3 on Psalm 1, this term means "fortunate" or "happy." The form of the sentence as well as the content seem anomalous. How could anyone become "happy" (i.e., living in a state of fulfillment) by killing innocent children? There is no satisfactory answer. Verse 9 might make more sense in the context of a world that was at times brutal, and that did not have the regard for children that the

> "The words of the psalmists are descriptive rather than prescriptive: they describe human reality . . . but they do not suggest that others should imitate or encourage the attitudes described." —Kathleen Farmer, "Psalms," in *Women's Bible Commentary*, Expanded Edition, ed. Carol A. Newsom and Sharon H. Ringe (Louisville, Ky.: Westminster John Knox Press, 1998), 149.

modern Western world has, but still this line cannot be made palatable. Even so, Christian interpreters should not whitewash the psalm. The psalmist seems to say that there is no acceptable world without Jerusalem as the capital, and anyone (i.e., the Babylonians) who attempts to create another kind of world deserves devastation.

God Alone, the Judge

Given the ending of Psalm 137, can this psalm serve as a model prayer for Christians in any way? Should the entire psalm be included in the church's liturgy (vv. 7–9 are typically removed from lectionary readings)? Despite the final lines of the psalm, the answer is yes, and even verses 7–9 can help guide Christian prayers. That is possible, however, only with the understanding that the main point of the psalm is not vengeance, but the memory of Zion. There is a proper place and time for a tenacity of faith that will not forget what has been meaningful at all costs. That tenacious faith and determination is at the heart of Psalm 137. Furthermore, history bears witness to a Jerusalem-centered faith that helped preserve Judaism and provide a foundation for Christianity. Jerusalem remains the picture of a holy city and inspires visions of a perfect world that is to come (Revelation 21–22).

We should also notice that the psalmist does not say that *he* will attempt to bring about retribution on his enemies. Instead his call,

"Remember, O LORD," indicates that God is the one who will repay Edom and Babylon. As one scholar has said, "The problem is not really that there is anger in Psalm 137. The real problem is that there is anger in every human heart." If we can learn to pray honestly, and in prayer give over hatred and wishes for vengeance to God, then perhaps prayer will bring a love for enemies that enables us to turn the other cheek to those who would strike us. This type of prayer reflects the faith that Israel developed eventually—a faith that God alone is in control of the universe, that God alone is judge. To relinquish control and to pray, even in anger, that God's will be done is the heart of model prayer (Matt. 6:10).

> "[This psalm] is an attempt, in the face of the most profound humiliation and helplessness, to suppress the primitive human lust for violence in one's heart, by surrendering *everything* to God." —Erich Zenger, *A God of Vengeance? Understanding the Psalms of Divine Wrath* (Louisville, Ky.: Westminster John Knox Press, 1996), 48.

A final note: Psalm 137 lies between Psalm 136 and Psalm 138, perhaps with good reason. As praise to Yahweh, the refrain of both those psalms is, "His steadfast love endures forever." Perhaps the placement of Psalm 137 speaks to the memory of the presence of God. When the waters of Babylon meet our lives, when we sit and weep, when we are tormented and angry, when we remember what was lost and cry out for justice, even then, though by our eyes unseen, God's love surrounds us.

? Questions for Reflection

1. What makes the desire for justice so compelling?
2. Memories can be powerful. Pictures, phrases, and even scents can trigger a memory, and what *is* remembered along with what *is not* remembered can affect behaviors and beliefs. Some social scientists define the human soul in connection with life-shaping memories. What does the psalmist want remembered in this psalm? Why?
3. The images of Babylon and Zion are used throughout the Bible. What do they represent? Where are the places of Babylon and Zion in your life?
4. Ephesians 4:26 exhorts, "Be angry but do not sin." How does this psalm influence your understanding of the Ephesians passage?

10 Psalm 22

The Psalms and Jesus Christ

Psalm 22, perhaps more than any other psalm, serves as a link to the story of Jesus' passion, the core of the Gospels. Of the thirteen references to the Old Testament in the passion stories, eight come from the book of Psalms, and five of those are from Psalm 22. All three psalms that provide material for the passion (Psalms 22; 31; 69) are laments spoken by an individual (or "prayers for help by an individual"). The Gospel writers seem to have identified this as an appropriate genre for the crucifixion account. The church in turn has read these laments in light of Jesus' suffering and death.

"My God, my God, why have you forsaken me?"

Uses in the Gospels

The best-known connection between the passion story and Psalm 22 is Jesus' so-called "cry of dereliction." Mark 15:34 (Matt. 27:46) gives the cry first in Jesus' native Aramaic, "Eloi, Eloi, lema sabachthani," and then translates, "My God, my God, why have you forsaken me?" This line is important both for its stark and honest complaint, and as an identification of the first line of Psalm 22. First lines of texts in

the ancient world often served as their titles. Just as today we identify a psalm by the number (i.e., the Twenty-third), the people of
Jesus' time (without chapter and verse divisions in their Bibles) recognized a particular psalm by the first line.

Using this type of recognition, perhaps the Gospel writers understood the cry by Jesus to be an identification with the whole experience recorded in Psalm 22. Supporting evidence is found by the way
the passion stories, particularly in Mark and Matthew, borrow other
verses from the psalm to outline the experience of Jesus on the cross.
Mark 15:29 (Matt. 27:39) implies the language of Psalm 22:7 in the
description of passersby at the crucifixion:

> All who see me mock at me;
> they make mouths at me, they shake their heads.

Matthew 27:43 also frames the taunts of the religious leaders with
an allusion to Psalm 22:8:

> Commit your cause to the LORD;
> let him deliver—
> let him rescue the one in whom he delights!

In all four Gospels (Mark 15:24; Matt. 27:35; Luke 23:34; John
19:24) the description of the soldiers' activity beneath the cross
draws on Psalm 22:18:

> they divide my clothes among themselves,
> and for my clothing they cast lots.

In addition to these examples, John 19:28 probably has Psalm 22:15
in mind when reporting that Jesus says, "I am thirsty" in order "to
fulfill scripture." The scripture fulfilled is most likely Psalm 22:15.

Does This Psalm Predict Jesus' Passion?

Why do the Gospels borrow so heavily from this particular psalm?
At points in the church's history, the answer has been simply that
Psalm 22 predicted Jesus' suffering; thus, the text was seen as proph-
esying events fulfilled in Jesus' passion. Adopting this perspective,
many in the church are unable to understand Psalm 22 apart from

the Gospels. However, a close comparison of the psalm with the passion narratives shows that the Gospel writers did not reproduce the language of Psalm 22 verbatim, or even in sequence. In their use, the psalmic verses were modified slightly in order to help shape the account of Jesus' death. Also, to view Psalm 22 as prophecy only in the strict sense of prediction denies the suffering of those many who prayed the psalm before Jesus. Jesus, in fact, stands in *their* tradition and in solidarity with them. That Jesus is a righteous sufferer seems to be one point the Gospels are making!

Ancient people did not write stories or present arguments as modern authors do. Western civilization tends to be overly concerned with questions of historical "proof"; when a story is told, one of the first questions we ask is, "Did it really happen this way?" followed by, "How do we know for sure?" For us, whether or not the story is considered "true," or for that matter has any real value, depends on its historical accuracy. Since the church affirms that the passion account is "true," and since that account describes Jesus' death using language that calls attention to Psalm 22, Psalm 22 understandably has been read as a prediction of the future. What else could explain the parallels in language?

> "Several details of the [passion] narrative appear to be the historicization of elements in the Psalm." —Lamar Williamson, Jr., *Mark,* Interpretation (Atlanta: John Knox Press, 1983), 275.

The Tradition of the Righteous Sufferer

The main question for ancient people, however, was not, "Is it historical?" but "Is it traditional? Does it reflect what has been known from the past?" That is, they asked if a current event or experience could stand in line with past experiences that were recognized as valid and meaningful. Using this idea, the Gospel writers understood Psalm 22, not so much as prediction, but as a lens through which to view the death of Jesus. How does one read the passion narratives in this light? As Mays suggests,

> That would be to follow the example of the apostles and the evangelists by using the psalm as a hermeneutical context. It may be that in

this way we glimpse something about the Christ and prayer and the relation between the two that might not be clear from other perspectives. (106)

Mays's comment about the apostles using Psalm 22 as a guide to interpreting (i.e., supplying a "hermeneutical context") Jesus' death is a reference to Hebrews 5:7, among other texts:

> In the days of his flesh, Jesus offered up prayers and supplications, with loud cries and tears, to him who was able to save him from death, and he was heard for his reverent submission.

> "[Jesus] gives all of his followers who are afflicted permission and encouragement to pray for help. He shows that faith includes holding the worst of life up to God."
> —James L. Mays, *Psalms*, Interpretation, 106.

Although the writer of Hebrews may not have had Psalm 22 in mind, the portrayal of Jesus at prayer as one who stands in the tradition of those who are afflicted, who suffer righteously, is consistent with this psalm. In the Garden of Gethsemane (Mark 14:32–42) and on the cross Jesus displayed this type of prayer. Psalm 22, and all prayers for help, do not so much prophesy as provide a context for Jesus' life and ministry.

The Structure

Psalm 22 is the prayer of complaint par excellence, and for that reason is particularly well suited to serve as the soil out of which the portrait of Jesus' suffering grew. This psalm has "an intensity and a comprehensiveness" that is almost unequaled among psalms of this type (Mays, 107). Part of this psalm's fervor comes from the structure. The psalm has two main parts: (1) a prayer for help in verses 1–21a; and (2) a song of praise in verses 21b–31. Both of these sections have two prominent divisions in which repetition of a main theme, sometimes with exact vocabulary, strengthens the complaint and praise. Note the repetition of themes and language in the divisions of the psalm in the following outline:

I. Prayer for Help (vv. 1–21a)
    A. Part One (vv. 1–11)
        1. "Why have you forsaken?" (vv. 1–2)

2. "*Yet you* are holy" (vv. 3–5)
3. "But I am a worm" (vv. 6–8)
4. "*Yet you* took me from womb" (vv. 9–10)
   "*Do not be far*" (v. 11)

B. Part Two (vv. 12–21a)
   1. "*Bulls* encircle me" (vv. 12–15)
   2. "*Dogs* around me" (vv. 16–18)
      "*Do not be far*" (v. 19a)
      "Come quickly" (v. 19b)
      "Deliver my soul" (v. 20)
      "from dog"
      "Save me" (v. 21a)
      "from *lion*"

II. Song of Praise (vv. 21b–31)
   A. Part One (vv. 21b–26)
      1. "I tell *brothers and sisters*" (vv. 22a–24)
      2. "Praise in *great congregation*" (v. 25)
      3. "*Poor/those who seek*" (v. 26)
   B. Part Two (vv. 27–31)
      1. "*Ends of the earth*" (vv. 27–28)
      2. "*All who sleep in the earth*" (vv. 29–31)

The sets of repetitions make the themes of petition and praise particularly strong. Notice that the two parts of the petition (vv. 1–11; 12–21a) conclude with the request, "Do not be far." The first section of the petition (vv. 1–11) itself has duplication in the alternating prayers of complaint and description of persecution (vv. 1–2; 6–8) and statements of confidence (vv. 3–5; 9–11). Both statements of confidence have "yet you" in their first line (vv. 3, 9). The second half of the prayer for help (vv. 12–21a) has two sections that begin with a description of enemies using animal imagery (bulls, dogs), and the petition concludes with another (lion).

The song of praise in verses 21b–31 also has two parts with repeated themes. As the song moves to an end, the circle of those who praise God becomes wider: from the congregation of Israel (vv. 22,

> "At this point, he is not so much afflicted by his physical sufferings; on the contrary, he suffers much more from . . . his own feeling . . . that God has broken off [God's] relationship with him, and that, in consequence, he is hoping for God in vain. The real sting of his suffering is the strain on his faith." —Artur Weiser, *The Psalms*, Old Testament Library, 222.

23, 25) to "all families of the nations" (v. 27) and "all who sleep in the earth" (v. 29).

The Power of the Psalm

Though the complex and repetitive development of themes and language contributes to its impact, the uniqueness of Psalm 22 comes from a mountain of unparalleled vocabulary that communicates both plight and confidence. The opening line, "My God, my God, why have you forsaken me?" sets the tone for the whole. The person who speaks is part of the chosen people who have praised God for generations (vv. 3–5), and who have witnessed God's salvation time and again. The God who created the universe is Israel's God and "my God" yet at the present moment God is "far away" (vv. 1, 11, 19), and that makes deliverance seem impossible. "I am a worm," "scorned," "despised" all

Want to Know More?

About citations of psalms in the New Testament? See Bernhard W. Anderson, *Out of the Depths: The Psalms Speak for Us Today* (Philadelphia: Westminster Press, 1983), 243–45.

About the concept of the righteous sufferer? See Horst Dietrich Preuss, *Old Testament Theology*, vol. 2, Old Testament Library (Louisville, Ky.: Westminster John Knox Press, 1996), 141–46.

About the Septuagint? See Celia Brewer Marshall, *A Guide through the Old Testament* (Louisville, Ky.: Westminster John Knox Press, 1989), 20; J. Alberto Soggin, *Introduction to the Old Testament*, 3d ed., Old Testament Library (Louisville, Ky.: Westminster John Knox Press, 1989),

express a dire situation. The animal metaphors are typical of the psalms. They reflect the sinister nature of enemies and may also suggest the presence of demonic forces. Psalm 22 contains a larger collection of this type of references than any other psalm. They draw images of being hunted (vv. 16, 20) and victimized by wild (v. 21) and powerful beasts (v. 12).

There is a disputed line related to the animal imagery that deserves some special comment. Verse 16b in Hebrew reads literally, "like a lion my hands and feet." The translators of the New Jewish Publication Society Version understand this to mean, "like lions [they maul] my hands and feet." The NRSV takes the verse to mean that the hands have shriveled; therefore, they look like the feet of a lion. However, the Greek translation of the Hebrew (the Septuagint) reads, "They have pierced my hands and feet." Early Christians read primarily from the Greek version, and they took this line as a reference to Jesus' suffering in crucifixion. As Mays notes, however, this verse is not one the Gospels borrow in their accounts of Jesus' passion. This may mean the evangelists and those before them who first told the story did not know this translation of the line (110–111). As the notes in the NRSV indicate, the verse is difficult to interpret, and no solution is fully satisfactory.

A Psalm of Gratitude

Verses 21b–31 shift the mood and genre from a plea for help to thanksgiving for help already received. The afflicted person has been delivered and now enters the sanctuary to offer formal worship for this renewed state. The person who gives thanks does so in the midst of a congregation of like-minded faithful ("brothers and sisters"; v. 22). The psalmist is identified with "the great congregation" (v. 25), which is defined further as "those who fear" (v. 25) and "the poor" (v. 26). "Poor" here translates the Hebrew word *aniwim* which can also be rendered "afflicted." Here, poverty does not refer to an economic condition, but to the state of the heart. The poor are those who submit themselves to God's rule, who seek the Lord with all their hearts, who "do not rely on their own insight" (Prov. 3:5). The poor are not a distinct, separate group but a group that comes to be understood as the true Israel nonetheless. As one from this group, the speaker of the psalm was taunted, "let him [the LORD] rescue the one in whom he delights" (v. 8). After the rescue, the thanksgiving meal hinted at in verse 26 is a celebration of the faithfulness of the psalmist and the *aniwim*.

A Psalm of Universal Praise

> "Everyone—everywhere, of every condition, in every time—will join in the worship of those who recognize and rejoice that universal sovereignty belongs to the LORD."
> —James L. Mays, *Psalms*, Interpretation, 112.

The second portion of the thanksgiving song (vv. 27–31) widens the congregation in amazing ways. "All the ends of the earth" and "all the families of the nations" shall worship God (v. 27). The universal rule of the Lord assumed here (v. 28) is much like that of the enthronement psalms (Psalms 47; 93; 95–99). Not only will the Lord rule over the nations, but all the nations will worship as part of God's people (Ps. 47:9). Perhaps more surprising, those "who sleep in the earth" will bow before the Lord (v. 29). This line is difficult to translate, and it does not seem to mean those already dead, but instead those "in the throes of death" (Mays, 113). Whether or not this interpretation is correct, a profound change has taken place in the thought world of the Psalms. Normally, those who are dying, or who have already died, are believed to be outside the realm of God's rule, and therefore they do not praise God (see Ps. 6:5). Here, even the nearly departed have come under the rule of the divine King.

One like a Savior

Who is the individual who spoke this psalm? That question of course cannot be answered with certainty. The psalm contains the words of one afflicted, whose cause is 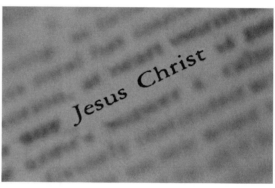 committed to the Lord, and who is vindicated. To claim that Jesus was the first to recite the psalm is unfair, but the work is almost tailor-made for his experience of suffering and for his role in the worldwide rule of God. As Mays observes, the universal context at the end of Psalm 22 suggests that not just any Israelite could have spoken these words (113). The only Old Testament figures capable of serving as a messenger to the nations as the psalm suggests are the Davidic king (the "anointed" or messiah) and the servant of Isaiah 42:1–4; 49:1–6; 52:13–53:12. Christian faith has as a central claim the belief that Jesus of Nazareth fulfilled the role of both of these. For that reason, to read Psalm 22 as the words of Jesus can be appropriate. Seeing Jesus' suffering and his role as "light to the nations" in the psalm links one to the congregation of the faithful, of those who rely on God. Psalm 22 encourages believers to seek God as they enter into fellowship with Christ, the one who spoke for and became one of the *aniwim* for the sake of us all.

? Questions for Reflection

1. This is a psalm that asks for help and offers praise. What kinds of help are sought by the psalmist? What kinds of praise are offered?

What would cause you to link a cry for help with an offering of praise?

2. This unit explains how passages from the Old Testament could have shaped the New Testament, but also how knowledge of the New Testament can influence the understanding of the Old Testament. What would you say to someone who tells you that Psalm 22 is describing the death of Jesus?

3. In this psalm, God is described as being both near and far. How can both be so? When God seems far away, what helps you sense God's closeness?

4. There is an interesting universal flavor to this psalm; even those dead or nearly dead will worship God. What do you think it means that "all the ends of the earth shall . . . turn to the LORD?"

Bibliography

Achtemeier, Paul J., ed. *Harper's Bible Dictionary.* San Francisco: Harper & Row, 1985.

Anderson, Bernhard W. *Out of the Depths: The Psalms Speak for Us Today.* Rev. and expanded ed. Philadelphia: Westminster Press, 1983.

Buechner, Frederick. *Wishful Thinking: A Theological ABC.* New York: Harper & Row, 1973.

Marshall, Celia Brewer. *A Guide through the Old Testament.* Louisville, Ky.: John Knox Press, 1989.

Mays, James L. *Psalms.* Interpretation: A Bible Commentary for Teaching and Preaching. Louisville, Ky.: John Knox Press, 1994.

Norris, Kathleen. *The Psalms.* New York: Riverhead Books, 1997.

Thompson, Marjorie J. *Soul Feast: An Invitation to the Christian Spiritual Life.* Louisville, Ky.: John Knox Press, 1995.

Weiser, Artur. *The Psalms, A Commentary.* Old Testament Library. Philadelphia: Westminster Press, 1962.

Interpretation Bible Studies
Leader's Guide

Interpretation Bible Studies (IBS), for adults and older youth, are flexible, attractive, easy-to-use, and filled with solid information about the Bible. IBS helps Christians discover the guidance and power of the scriptures for living today. Perhaps you are leading a church school class, a mid-week Bible study group, or a youth group meeting, or simply using this in your own personal study. Whatever the setting may be, we hope you find this *Leader's Guide* helpful. Since every context and group is different, this *Leader's Guide* does not presume to tell you how to structure Bible study for your situation. Instead, the *Leader's Guide* seeks to offer choices—a number of helpful suggestions for leading a successful Bible study using IBS.

> "The church that no longer hears the essential message of the Scriptures soon ceases to understand what it is for and is open to be captured by the dominant religious philosophy of the moment." —James D. Smart, *The Strange Silence of the Bible in the Church: A Study in Hermeneutics* (Philadelphia: Westminster Press, 1970), 10.

How Should I Teach IBS?

1. Explore the Format

There is a wealth of information in IBS, perhaps more than you can use in one session. In this case, more is better. IBS has been designed to give you a well-stocked buffet of content and teachable insights. Pick and choose what suits your group's needs. Perhaps you will want to split units into two or more sessions, or combine units into a single session. Perhaps you will decide to use only a portion of a

"The more we bring to the Bible, the more we get from the Bible." —William Barclay, *A Beginner's Guide to the New Testament* (Louisville, Ky.: Westminster John Knox Press, 1995), vii.

unit and then move on to the next unit. *There is not a structured theme or teaching focus to each unit that must be followed for IBS to be used.* Rather, IBS offers the flexibility to adjust to whatever suits your context.

A recent survey of both professional and volunteer church educators revealed that their number one concern was that Bible study materials be teacher-friendly. IBS is, indeed teacher-friendly in two important ways. First, since IBS provides abundant content and a flexible design, teachers can shape the lessons creatively, responding to the needs of the group and employing a wide variety of teaching methods. Second, those who wish more specific suggestions for planning the sessions can find them at the Westminster John Knox Press Web site (www.wjkbooks.com). Here, you can access a study guide with teaching suggestions for each IBS unit as well as helpful quotations, selections from Bible dictionaries and encyclopedias, and other teaching helps.

IBS is also not only teacher-friendly, it is also discussion-friendly. Given the opportunity, most adults and young people relish the chance to talk about the kind of issues raised in IBS. The secret, then, is to determine what works with your group, what will get them to talk. Several good methods for stimulating discussion are presented in this *Leader's Guide,* and once you learn your group, you can apply one of these methods and get the group discussing the Bible and its relevance in their lives.

The format of every IBS unit consists of several features:

a. Body of the Unit. This is the main content, consisting of interesting and informative commentary on the passage and scholarly insight into the biblical text and its significance for Christians today.

b. Sidebars. These are boxes that appear scattered throughout the body of the unit, with maps, photos, quotations, and intriguing ideas. Some sidebars can be identified quickly by a symbol, or icon, that helps the reader know what type of information can be found in that sidebar. There are icons for illustrations, key terms, pertinent quotes, and more.

c. Want to Know More? Each unit includes a "Want to Know

More?" section that guides learners who wish to dig deeper and consult other resources. If your church library does not have the resources mentioned, you can look up the information in other standard Bible dictionaries, encyclopedias, and handbooks, or you can find much of this information at the Geneva Press Web site (see page 112).

d. Questions for Reflection. The unit ends with questions to help the learners think more deeply about the biblical passage and its pertinence for today. These questions are provided as examples only, and teachers are encouraged both to develop their own list of questions and to gather questions from the group. These discussion questions do not usually have specific "correct" answers. Again, the

> "The trick is to make the Bible our book."
> —Duncan S. Ferguson, *Bible Basics: Mastering the Content of the Bible* (Louisville, Ky.: Westminster John Knox Press, 1995), 3.

flexibility of IBS allows you to use these questions at the end of the group time, at the beginning, interspersed throughout, or not at all.

2. Select a Teaching Method

Here are ten suggestions. The format of IBS allows you to choose what direction you will take as you plan to teach. Only you will know how your lesson should best be designed for your group. Some adult groups prefer the lecture method, while others prefer a high level of free ranging discussion. Many youth groups like interaction, activity, the use of music, and the chance to talk about their own experiences and feelings. Here is a list of a few possible approaches. Let your own creativity add to the list!

a. Let's Talk about What We've Learned. In this approach, all group members are requested to read the scripture passage and the IBS unit before the group meets. Ask the group members to make notes about the main issues, concerns, and questions they see in the passage. When the group meets, these notes are collected, shared, and discussed. This method depends, of course, on the group's willingness to do some "homework."

b. What Do We Want and Need to Know? This approach begins by having the whole group read the scripture passage together.

Then, drawing from your study of the IBS, you, as the teacher, write on a board or flip chart two lists:

(1) Things we should know to better understand this passage" (content information related to the passage, for example, historical insights about political contexts, geographical landmarks, economic nuances, etc.] and

(2) Four or five "important issues we should talk about regarding this passage" [with implications for today- how the issues in the biblical context continue into today, for example, issues of idolatry or fear]. Allow the group to add to either list, if they wish, and use the lists to lead into a time of learning, reflection, and discussion. This approach is suitable for those settings where there is little or no advanced preparation by the students.

> "Although small groups can meet for many purposes and draw upon many different resources, the one resource which has shaped the life of the Church more than any other throughout its long history has been the Bible." —Roberta Hestenes, *Using the Bible in Groups* (Philadelphia: Westminster Press, 1983), 14.

c. Hunting and Gathering.   Start the unit by having the group read the scripture passage together. Then divide the group into smaller clusters (perhaps having as few as one person), each with a different assignment. Some clusters can discuss one or more of the "Questions for Reflection." Others can look up key terms or people in a Bible dictionary or track down other biblical references found in the body of the unit. After the small clusters have had time to complete their tasks, gather the entire group again and lead them through the study material, allowing each cluster to contribute what it learned.

d. From Question Mark to Exclamation Point.   This approach begins with contemporary questions and then moves to the biblical content as a response to those questions. One way to do this is for you to ask the group, at the beginning of the class, a rephrased version of one or more of the "Questions for Reflection" at the end of the study unit. For example, one of the questions at the end of the unit on Exodus 3:1–4:17 in the IBS *Exodus* volume reads,

> Moses raised four protests, or objections, to God's call. Contemporary people also raise objections to God's call. In what ways are these similar to Moses' protests? In what ways are they different?

This question assumes familiarity with the biblical passage about

Moses, so the question would not work well before the group has explored the passage. However, try rephrasing this question as an opening exercise; for example:

> Here is a thought experiment: Let's assume that God, who called people in the Bible to do daring and risky things, still calls people today to tasks of faith and courage. In the Bible, God called Moses from a burning bush and called Isaiah in a moment of ecstatic worship in the Temple. How do you think God's call is experienced by people today? Where do you see evidence of people saying "yes" to God's call? When people say "no" or raise an objection to God's call, what reasons do they give (to themselves, to God)?

Posing this or a similar question at the beginning will generate discussion and raise important issues, and then it can lead the group into an exploration of the biblical passage as a resource for thinking even more deeply about these questions.

e. Let's Go to the Library. From your church library, your pastor's library, or other sources, gather several good commentaries on the book of the Bible you are studying. Among the trustworthy commentaries are those in the Interpretation series (John Knox Press) and the Westminster Bible Companion series (Westminster John Knox Press). Divide your group into smaller clusters and give one commentary to each cluster (one or more of the clusters can be given the IBS volume instead of a full-length commentary). Ask each cluster to read the biblical passage you are studying and then to read the section of the commentary that covers that passage (if your group is large, you may want to make photocopies of the commentary material with proper permission, of course). The task of each cluster is to name the two or three most important insights they discover about the biblical passage by reading and talking together about the commentary material. When you reassemble the larger group to share these insights, your group will not only gain a variety of insights about the passage but also a sense that differing views of the same text are par for the course in biblical interpretation.

f. Working Creatively Together. Begin with a creative group task, tied to the main thrust of the study. For example, if the study is on the Ten Commandments, a parable, or a psalm, have the group rewrite the Ten Commandments, the parable, or the psalm in contemporary language. If the passage is an epistle, have the group write a letter to their own congregation. Or if the study is a narrative, have the group role-play the characters in the story or write a page describing the story from the point of view of one of the characters. After completion of the task, read and discuss the biblical passage, asking for interpretations and applications from the group and tying in IBS material as it fits the flow of the discussion.

g. Singing Our Faith. Begin the session by singing (or reading) together a hymn that alludes to the biblical passage being studied (or to the theological themes in the passage). Most hymnals have an index of scriptural allusions. For example, if you are studying the unit from the IBS volume on Psalm 121, you can sing "I to the Hills Will Lift My Eyes," "Sing Praise to God, Who Reigns Above," or another hymn based on Psalm 121. Let the group reflect on the thoughts and feelings evoked by the hymn, then move to the biblical passage, allowing the biblical text and the IBS material to underscore, clarify, refine, and deepen the discussion stimulated by the hymn. If you are ambitious, you may ask the group to write a new hymn at the end of the study! [Many hymnals have indexes in the back or companion volumes that help the user match hymns to scripture passages or topics.]

h. Fill in the Blanks. In order to help the learners focus on the content of the biblical passage, at the beginning of the session ask each member of the group to read the biblical passage and fill out a brief questionnaire about the details of the passage (provide a copy for each learner or write the questions on the board). For example, if you are studying the unit in the IBS *Matthew* volume on Matthew 22:1–14, the questionnaire could include questions such as the following:

—In this story, Jesus compares the kingdom of heaven to what?

—List the various responses of those who were invited to the king's banquet but who did not come.

—When his invitation was rejected, how did the king feel? What did the king do?

—In the second part of the story, when the king saw a man at the banquet without a wedding garment, what did the king say? What did the man say? What did the king do?

—What is the saying found at the end of this story?

Gather the group's responses to the questions perhaps encourage discussion. Then lead the group through the IBS material helping the learners to understand the meanings of these details and the significance of the passage for today. Feeling creative? Instead of a fill-in-the blanks questionnaire, create a crossword puzzle from names and words in the biblical passage.

i. Get the Picture. In this approach, stimulate group discussion by incorporating a painting, photograph, or other visual object into the lesson. You can begin by having the group examine and comment on this visual or you can introduce the visual later in the lesson—it depends on the object used. If, for example, you are studying the unit Exodus 3:1–4:17 in the IBS *Exodus* volume, you may want to view Paul Koli's very colorful painting *The Burning Bush*. Two sources for this painting are *The Bible Through Asian Eyes*, edited by Masao Takenaka and Ron O'Grady (National City, Calif.: Pace Publishing Co., 1991), and *Imaging the Word: An Arts and Lectionary Resource,* vol. 3, edited by Susan A. Blain (Cleveland: United Church Press, 1996).

j. Now Hear This. Especially if your class is large, you may want to use the lecture method. As the teacher, you prepare a presentation on the biblical passage, using as many resources as you have available plus your own experience, but following the content of the IBS unit as a guide. You can make the lecture even more lively by asking the learners at various points along the way to refer to the visuals and quotes found in the "sidebars." A place can be made for questions (like the ones at the end of the unit)— either at the close of the lecture or at strategic points along the way.

> "It is . . . important to call a Bible study group back to what the text being discussed actually says, especially when an individual has gotten off on some tangent."
> —Richard Robert Osmer, *Teaching for Faith: A Guide for Teachers of Adult Classes* (Louisville, Ky.: Westminster John Knox Press, 1992), 71.

3. Keep These Teaching Tips in Mind

There are no surefire guarantees for a teaching success. However, the following suggestions can increase the chances for a successful study:

a. Always Know Where the Group Is Headed. Take ample time beforehand to prepare the material. Know the main points of the study, and know the destination. Be flexible, and encourage discussion, but don't lose sight of where you are headed.

b. Ask Good Questions; Don't Be Afraid of Silence. Ideally, a discussion blossoms spontaneously from the reading of the scripture. But more often than not, a discussion must be drawn from the group members by a series of well-chosen questions. After asking each question, give the group members time to answer. Let them think, and don't be threatened by a season of silence. Don't feel that every question must have an answer, and that as leader, you must supply every answer. Facilitate discussion by getting the group members to cooperate with each other. Sometimes, the original question can be restated. Sometimes it is helpful to ask a follow-up question like "What makes this a hard question to answer?"

Ask questions that encourage explanatory answers. Try to avoid questions that can be answered simply "Yes" or "No." Rather than asking, "Do you think Moses was frightened by the burning bush?" ask, "What do you think Moses was feeling and experiencing as he stood before the burning bush?" If group members answer with just one word, ask a follow-up question like "Why do you think this is so?" Ask questions about their feelings and opinions, mixed within questions about facts or details. Repeat their responses or restate their response to reinforce their contributions to the group.

> "Studies of learning reveal that while people remember approximately 10% of what they hear, they remember up to 90% of what they say. Therefore, to increase the amount of learning that occurs, increase the amount of talking about the Bible which each member does."—Roberta Hestenes, *Using the Bible in Groups* (Philadelphia: Westminster Press, 1983), 17.

Most studies can generate discussion by asking open-ended questions. Depending on the group, several types of questions can work. Some groups will respond well to content questions that can be answered from reading the IBS comments or the biblical passage. Others will respond well to questions about feelings or thoughts. Still others will respond to questions that challenge them to new thoughts or that may not have exact answers. Be sensitive to the group's dynamic in choosing questions.

Some suggested questions are: What is the point of the passage? Who are the main characters? Where is the tension in the story? Why does it say (this)_____, and not (that) _____? What raises questions for you? What terms need defining? What are the new ideas? What doesn't make sense? What bothers or troubles you about this passage? What keeps you from living the truth of this passage?

c. Don't Settle for the Ordinary. There is nothing like a surprise. Think of special or unique ways to present the ideas of the study. Upset the applecart of the ordinary. Even though the passage may be familiar, look for ways to introduce suspense. Remember that a little mystery can capture the imagination. Change your routine.

Along with the element of surprise, humor can open up a discussion. Don't be afraid to laugh. A well-chosen joke or cartoon may present the central theme in a way that a lecture would have stymied.

Sometimes a passage is too familiar. No one speaks up because everyone feels that all that could be said has been said. Choose an unfamiliar translation from which to read, or if the passage is from a Gospel, compare the story across two or more Gospels and note differences. It is amazing what insights can be drawn from seeing something strange in what was thought to be familiar.

d. Feel Free to Supplement the IBS Resources with Other Material. Consult other commentaries or resources. Tie in current events with the lesson. Scour newspapers or magazines for stories that touch on the issues of the study. Sometimes the lyrics of a song, or a section of prose from a well-written novel will be just the right seasoning for the study.

e. And Don't Forget to Check the Web. You can download a free study guide from our Web site (www.wjkbooks.com). Each study guide includes several possibilities for applying the teaching methods suggested above for individual IBS units.

f. Stay Close to the Biblical Text. Don't forget that the goal is to learn the Bible. Return to the text again and again. Avoid making the mistake of reading the passage only at the beginning of the study, and then wandering away to comments on top of comments

> "The Bible is literature, but it is much more than literature. It is the holy book of Jews and Christians, who find there a manifestation of God's presence." —Kathleen Norris, *The Psalms* (New York: Riverhead Books, 1997), xxii.

from that point on. Trust in the power and presence of the Holy Spirit to use the truths of the passage to work within the lives of the study participants.

What If I Am Using IBS in Personal Bible Study?

If you are using IBS in your personal Bible study, you can experiment and explore a variety of ways. You may choose to read straight through the study without giving any attention to the sidebars or other features. Or you may find yourself interested in a question or unfamiliar with a key term, and you can allow the sidebars," "Want to Know More?" and "Questions for Reflection" to lead you into deeper learning on these issues. Perhaps you will want to have a few commentaries or a Bible dictionary available to pursue what interests you. As was suggested in one of the teaching methods above, you may want to begin with the questions at the end, and then read the Bible passage followed by the IBS material. Trust the IBS resources to provide good and helpful information, and then follow your interests!

Want to Know More?

About leading Bible study groups? See Roberta Hestenes, *Using the Bible in Groups* (Philadelphia: Westminster Press, 1983).

About basic Bible content? See Duncan S. Ferguson, *Bible Basics: Mastering the Content of the Bible* (Louisville, Ky.: Westminster John Knox Press, 1995); William M. Ramsay, *The Westminster Guide to the Books of the Bible* (Louisville, Ky.: Westminster John Knox Press, 1994).

About the development of the Bible? See John Barton, *How the Bible Came to Be* (Louisville, Ky.: Westminster John Knox Press, 1997).

About the meaning of difficult terms? See Donald K. McKim, *Westminster Dictionary of Theological Terms* (Louisville, Ky.: Westminster John Knox Press, 1996); Paul J. Achtemeier, *Harper's Bible Dictionary* (San Francisco: Harper & Row, 1985).

To download a free IBS study guide,
visit our Web site at www.wjkbooks.com.